Confessions of a Chronic Depressive

A RECORD OF STRUGGLE AND PERSEVERANCE

Laura Grace Dykes

Copyright © 2016 Laura Grace Dykes

N-COURAGE Resources

Published by N-Courage Resources.

All rights reserved. No part of this book may be reproduced without permission from the author, except by a reviewer quoting brief passages in a review; nor may any part of this book be reproduced, stored in a retrieval system, or copied by mechanical photocopying, recording, or other means without written permission from the author.

Scripture taken from the HOLY BIBLE, NEW INTERNATIONAL VERSION®. NIV®. Copyright © 1973, 1978, 1984 by International Bible Society. Used by permission of Zondervan. All rights reserved worldwide.

Scripture quotations from THE MESSAGE. Copyright © by Eugene H. Peterson 1993, 1994, 1995, 1996, 2000, 2001, 2002. Used by permission of NavPress. All rights reserved. Represented by Tyndale House Publishers, Inc.

This book is dedicated to anyone who suffers from depression. Today and every day, if no one else is, know that I'm sending you love and strength. You are irreplaceable.

Table of Contents

Acknowledgments 1

Introduction 3

Chapter 1 - It Is Happening Again 5

Chapter 2 - What to Do with What You're Given 7

Chapter 3 - When Depression Makes You Lash Out 13

Chapter 4 - Stolen Identity 17

Chapter 5 - What about Your Friends? 19

Chapter 6 - Anxiety, My Old Friend 23

Chapter 7 - Trying to Find Pleasure
When You Feel Nothing but Pain 27

Chapter 8 - Talking to Myself 31

Chapter 9 - Crying Out to God 35

Chapter 10 - For My Daughter 39

Chapter 11- Standing Up to Stigma 43

Chapter 12 - On Suicidal Ideation 47

Chapter 13 - The Tragic Beauty of Depression 51

Chapter 14 - When I Started Reciting the Rosary 55

Chapter 15 - I Love Myself! 59

Chapter 16 - Changing Vows 63

Chapter 17 - The Battle of Self-Harm 67

Chapter 18 - Saying Good-bye, Part 1 73

Chapter 19 - Saying Good-bye, Part 2 75

Chapter 20 - How to Build a Life around Depression 77

Epilogue: Who I Am 83

Acknowledgments

God gave me life, and then when I tried to end it, He saved me. Thanks are not enough, but, miraculously, God's grace is.

I want to thank my parents and my sister—David and Cindy Dykes and Jenni Holman. My first family, the people who showed me unconditional love when I was shining brightest and when I was drowning in darkness. The three of them have saved my life more than once, and no one time in my life has meant more to me than when they came to (and stayed beside) my hospital bedside after my suicide attempt. I felt unworthy of life or love, and they refused to let me stay that way. They showed me my value, my strength, and my capacity for love.

I have also been ridiculously blessed with some of the most beautiful friends any person on earth could have. There are so many, but the five who have made the most impact on my adult life are Abby Crawford, Amanda Flynn, Amanda Klinger, Denesha Alexander, and Steve Sexton. Each of them has seen me in pretty bad shape and hasn't backed away. They have all supported and continue to support me on my journey. Friendship is one of God's greatest gifts to us, and I wouldn't trade these friends or the lessons they have taught me for anything.

Finally, I must thank my husband and my daughter—Jim and Ada Liner. Jim supports me in every way that a best friend, husband, and partner should. We may not believe in soul mates, but we love and cherish the commitment we have made to be each other's life partner. I wouldn't want to take this journey with anyone else. And my daughter. My reason to fight. She is the joy of my life and my motivation to hope. She teaches me daily about love and compassion. I can never repay either of them for giving me such a beautiful life.

Without all of you, I certainly would not be here. Thank you for showing me that I am valuable, loved, and strong. Thank you for giving me the courage to write, but, more importantly, thank you for giving me the courage to live.

Excerpted from the author's blog, *Confessions of a Chronic Depressive: A Record of Struggle and Perseverance*. Visit www.ConfessionsOfAChronicDepressive.wordpress.com.

Introduction

At the beginning of October 2015, I was in a tough spot. I was out of medication, without a doctor, and beginning to find daily life more and more difficult. I was fragile, on edge, fatigued, isolated. I was spending more and more time in mental and emotional pain. I was facing a breakdown, and it seemed inevitable. I was afraid, but I was also angry.

Over the past 15 years, I had dedicated myself to either regaining or maintaining my mental health, and after all the success, I was going to lose the fight because I didn't have medication. All of my hard work, all of my daily blessings, and I wanted to kill myself. It wasn't fair; it wasn't right. I knew, when I could see beyond the haze of my depression, that I was not alone, that I was lovable, that I deserved better, but I hated the fact that I could not feel that truth every day.

So I began writing. I have journaled quite a bit throughout my life, but I didn't want to just record the depths to which my depression took me. I wanted to record the fight because I have fought hard over the past 15 years. I knew that if it all became too much, if I didn't get help, I was going lose; I was going to give in. So I went public. I decided to tell my story, share the lessons I had learned, and try to support anyone else who felt how I felt. And if I lost the fight, I wanted to have left behind some proof that I had tried. In the process, it gave me a chance to review the past 15 years of my life, see myself as the fighter I wanted to be, and acknowledge my utter success at fighting a disease that was trying to kill me.

Writing my blog—*Confessions of a Chronic Depressive* (www.ConfessionsOfAChronicDepressive.wordpress.com)—saved my life. Writing publicly forced me to find help and get back on medication. Writing helped me get through the tough days that I continued to face as I began healing from being on the verge of a full-blown suicidal episode. Writing helped me remember all of the things I had learned over the past 15 years, and it gave me a better understanding of myself. The self-reflection has been cathartic, the openness has been healing, and the honesty has been life changing.

This book is a collection of posts from my blog published between October 2015 and January 2016, with two new posts written in March 2016 as I worked on completing the manuscript. In this collection you will find plenty of information about me, but more importantly, you will either get an inside look at chronic depression or you will find a friend who knows the pain you experience. If I have learned anything in my struggle with depression, it is that this disease is tireless and requires tireless effort on your part. Fight every moment you can, and when you can't fight, hold on and find help. You are not alone. You are valuable. You are brave. You are irreplaceable, and your story deserves to be heard.

1
It Is Happening Again

IT IS HAPPENING AGAIN. I'm facing my biggest fear. Again. And I really don't know whether I can do it. My life hangs in the balance. Depression threatens to swallow me for good—force my hand—make me believe that I am broken beyond repair and *must* end it.

I was diagnosed with major depression in 2001 at the age of 19 after a suicide attempt that landed me in the hospital for 48 hours. My guess is that I was depressed for more than a year before my diagnosis. Since then I have had four more distinct depressive episodes. My struggles have also included agoraphobia, panic attacks, and generalized anxiety. Medical research finds that the more episodes you have the more likely you are to keep getting depressed. With five episodes under my belt in only 15 years, full recovery seems unlikely, and my big fear is that depression will lead me back to suicide. There it is. The thing I feel so afraid to even say: I am terribly afraid of killing myself because the disease I have makes me believe that it is the right answer.

Yesterday was a bad day for me. I cried for roughly nine hours, unable to eat or sleep. Nausea, headache, diarrhea, despair, hopelessness, fear. Finally I texted my husband to come home from work because I could no longer be alone. My sick brain was talking to me, intermittently whispering and screaming the same garbage it has been trying to get me to believe for the past 15 years. And no matter how much therapy I have, that voice is never really gone. Maybe it never will be. Because depression is more than just suicide. It will kill you slowly, smothering out all the light and leaving nothingness.

So how do I face this again? How do I face the probability of a lifelong struggle with depression? One day at a time and with lots of support. My entire life is dedicated to fighting my illness. It is my greatest luxury and I refuse to take advantage of it. My job is to stay healthy and maintain balance. My purpose is to help others like me somehow. I might truly be at the start of another episode or maybe I can fight it off. We'll see. But I am a fighter, and I want everyone who faces depression to fight. I want to be open, real, honest, and helpful.

Yesterday I looked in the mirror with tears streaming down my face and said over and over, "I am not alone." And yet I felt nothing but pain. Today I can fight. So I will. And if I'm headed back into the pit, this will be the record of my fight.

2

What to Do with What You're Given

DEPRESSION IS VERY ISOLATING; HOWEVER, CARING FOR A DEEPLY DEPRESSED PERSON IS ALSO ISOLATING. You fear you can't tell anyone what your loved one is struggling with because it is often very private. You feel you must constantly remain strong for fear of letting down your loved one. You feel lost because you cannot understand what your loved one is going through. To be honest, I don't know what caretakers go through. You walk a separate journey perhaps as difficult as the depression itself. Only those who have walked in your shoes can begin to understand your suffering.

What I do know, though, is that you have the opportunity to make a major impact on the world by saving a life. I have tried to think of a few things that have made an impact on me—there are so many more—and condense them into seven tips. This is not exhaustive, by any means, but merely an encouragement to you to keep standing beside your depressed friend, parent, sibling, child, etc.

1. *Physically Be There*

In 2001 I called my parents in the midst of taking roughly 70 Tylenol. I didn't tell them what I was doing, but I said I needed them, and they immediately drove more than two hours to physically be with me. They literally saved my life that day. And they stayed with me. For weeks after, my mother spent all but a few hours a week with me—including sharing a bed. During her hours off, my dad was with me. I was never alone. Sometimes being physically present is soothing, sometimes it is life saving. Don't hesitate to sit in silence. Don't be put off by the tears. Sometimes your physical presence is enough.

2. *Figure Out Your Priorities*

My first episode after marriage was my most suicidal since 2001. I had moved from Oklahoma to Washington, my husband was finishing his dissertation in the garage of the house we were sharing with a generous friend, and I was crumbling under the weight of isolation and the stresses of parenting a toddler. My husband kept thinking that if we could just hold on until he could finish his dissertation, then he could help me. He felt like he could better help me once he was done, so he had to finish writing first. But depression waits for no man. Once I began to practice my suicide plan, I told him I couldn't wait any longer. His priorities had to change. Writing had to wait because I couldn't. It isn't fair. But it may be necessary. My husband waited too long, and though he kept me from losing my life, I continued to sink into my worst episode in a decade. Don't put the depression of a loved one on the back burner. Depression is a slippery slope, and it is much harder to climb up than it is to slide down. Don't wait. Make recovery a priority at depression's earliest iteration. If you don't prioritize the health of your loved one, they probably won't either.

3. *Go to Great Lengths*

For a while I was a graduate student and first-year composition instructor at the University of Oklahoma. My third year there I was terribly anxious and again depressed. My future husband lived in Florida, and my parents lived in Texas. I was trying to continue my work as a student and teacher, trying to keep together the life I had worked hard to build, but I was falling apart. So my mother packed her bags and moved to my one-bedroom apartment in Oklahoma, leaving behind her husband, her home, her friends, and her livelihood. She stayed with me for six weeks, coming to campus with me, spending every anxious moment with me, talking me down from irrational panic, helping me move through desperation back to hope. You may not be able to drop your life and move to your loved one, but don't be afraid to go to great lengths to help. Make a difficult phone call, pay for counseling, make time for a vacation together, share a personal moment.

When I was in the hospital in 2001 after my suicide attempt, my father shared something with me when we had some time alone—the chorus to a then-popular country song about finding identity through the lens of loved ones when feeling lost. He recited it to me, looking me in my eyes with tears streaming down his face. And he told me it was true. If I didn't know who I was, they did, and they wouldn't stop fighting until I could see myself again too. He didn't travel far or spend money, but he opened up deep. He loved big and he gave me a gift of raw intimacy. Dig in and dig deep. Go places you've never gone before because, I promise, depression will take you there anyway. It's better if you're driving the bus.

4. Research and Encourage

Yesterday I began rereading a book called *The Singer* by Calvin Miller. My dad gave this book to me about three years ago; it's a long poem that imagines Jesus as a singer of the greatest song of the universe, and opens with Jesus finding His purpose as the singer and knowing the suffering that would come along with it. My parents and I are Christians, and our faith is a major foundation of our relationship. My dad also knows that I love poetry, especially 20th-century poetry, and that part of my personal struggle is maintaining a stable identity. So he gave me a book of poetry from 1975 about Jesus' understanding of existential torment. He listened to me, he thought about my interests, he racked his brain for ideas, and then he bought this book and gave it to me. "I love it!" I cried. I found meaning in my struggle, I found strength in my faith. Again, he dug deep, and he pulled something from his own past to share with me, encouraging me and strengthening our bond.

Don't be afraid to be active in your loved one's recovery. Ask about therapy and listen. Ask about the little things but also ask about the big things and listen. Read books about the diagnosis and the type of therapy being used to treat your loved one. Find media that has spoken to you in times of darkness and carefully weigh whether sharing it would strengthen your loved one. Always encourage your loved one to keep pushing. Just yesterday my dad emailed me: "Like Winston Churchill said, 'Nevah give up. Nevah! Nevah! Nevah!'" There is no such thing as standing still in depression. Even if I'm not moving, the depression is. If I can't swim, I must at least tread water because otherwise I'll drown. Keep the fight going through participation and encouragement.

5. *Show Interest*

I used to write poetry, especially during the depressed year before my diagnosis. However, I did continue to write for a time after my diagnosis. It was very therapeutic for me and made me feel special. It wasn't that great but it was meaningful to me. My family would listen to my poems and respond with questions probing the deep issues I addressed. They would engage me in one of the few things where I could find happiness. My mother doesn't even like poetry that much, but she engaged. My sister, an untouchable pillar of strength and success in my eyes at the time, once told me after a poetry reading, "I could never do something like that. You are so gifted." It was a revelation; in my darkest moment I was doing something that some stable people couldn't do.

She showed interest in my work, but more importantly, she showed interest in me. Sometimes I feel like those who love me most need me least because I am a burden. But when they showed interest in whatever I was able to be invested in, I felt as if I was contributing somehow to their lives.

6. Provide Affirmation

Friday, after my husband came home early from work, I asked him meekly, "Can you tell me why you need me?" I felt embarrassed and ashamed to be asking such a selfish question, but I couldn't remember why anyone needed me. I felt useless. Anything I actually did could be done by someone else. Jim immediately turned to face me, looked me straight in the eyes—tears welling up in his own—and said, "I am a better person with you in my life. I am different without you, and I want to be the person I am when I'm with you." Wow. He told me that no one could replace me in his eyes. I mattered because there is no one else who could do what I do in the way that I do it. I asked for affirmation, and he gave it. But it took me years to gain the courage to ask for affirmation of my existence. Don't wait for your loved one to ask, tell them why they matter to you, why they cannot be replaced. Tell them every chance you get that they are needed. Because depression makes it so easy to forget everything good. Don't just stop at "I love you." Say "I love you because _____." If you say it enough it will begin to stick, and one day they may actually believe it.

7. Support Yourself

Finally, find support for yourself as a caretaker. Talk to friends about your heartache and frustration, join support groups of other caretakers, or find a counselor of your own to help you process your thoughts and feelings. Don't deny yourself the support that you most definitely need while you care for your sick friend or family member. You will struggle, you will suffer, but hopefully you will find wellsprings of strength.

3

When Depression Makes You Lash Out

Sometimes when I'm really hurting I get vicious and lash out at those around me. I can see it, but instead of correcting it, I own it. I hold on to it tightly because I think I'm really as awful as I'm acting, and what I want is for people to see how terrible I am and save themselves by

running away. I think that all I can do is cause pain. I am nothing but a burden, and I want other people to see that "truth." It's like those movie scenes where an animal is being released into the wild, and the human caretaker has to act hateful toward it so that it will do what is best for itself and return to the wild. I think I'm saving you. When I'm really ill I feel as if I can only meaningfully contribute to the world by taking my wicked self out of it. This is a *lie*! I am not hostile or mean. You all send me texts, emails, and messages telling me you like me, but sometimes I still act out my pain—perform the hurt I feel. I want to encourage you to acknowledge this about yourself if it is true for you. But more importantly, I want you to recognize that you may be pushing people away, and this will not help you fight depression.
If you hurt, show it, but acknowledge what it really is. It's depression taking control. So here are two ideas for addressing negative behavior.

1. Recognize the Real Issue and Address It

I can't emphasize how important it is to recognize the roots of your actions. What is motivating you to be a jerk? This takes work. I spend a lot of time reflecting on my thoughts, feelings, and actions. I journal and talk to my husband. Depression makes you feel deeply, so I suggest thinking deeply about your feelings. Saturday morning my daughter came to get in bed with my husband and me. She immediately asked me a question about God followed by a question about heaven. My husband, an atheist and morning grouch, was frustrated. He didn't say or do anything, but I can read him really well. It pissed me off. I was angry at him. I got up and began slamming things around in the kitchen as

I made coffee and my daughter's breakfast. I even cursed at the toaster. My husband and I coarsely exchanged words, but then I began to reflect on why I was so angry.

It had nothing to do with my husband's atheism or his frustration at my exposing our daughter to Christianity. It's that I am currently struggling with feeling like I have my feet in two ponds—a Christian pond (my parents, church group, a few friends) and a secular pond (my husband, more friends). I had been holding on to that struggle, afraid to mention it anywhere but in my prayers. So I told my husband what I had been feeling, and the tears began to fall, but the fight was over and my anger was gone. I felt sad, yes, but also relieved. My anger could have put a wedge between my husband and me for the whole day, and my depression could have deepened the wedge over time. Our differing spiritualities is a big issue, but I won't let it ruin my marriage and family. My husband is an amazing partner and supports me completely—including my Christianity. I would be a fool to push him away, and when I saw how my depression was turning a real struggle into undue suffering I began to regain control. Maybe it sounds easy—it isn't. It takes a lot of practice, but it's worth it. Search for why you are hurting and refocus your attention on the real reason you're being combative.

2. Find Role Models

When you don't know how to act because you are hurting, focus on someone else—someone you can look up to. Not someone in an ivory tower, not someone you put on a pedestal. Choose someone who has overcome struggle and shown love to great extremes. Jesus is a good example whether or not you believe in His divinity. The way I see Jesus through the accounts in the Bible is as a radical preaching love over legalism and showing love despite suffering and alienation. Helen Keller has been a role model for me since I was a child. She faced tremendous struggle throughout her life and not only persevered but also flourished. It can even be people you know. I have two dear (but geographically distant) friends from growing up who I still text with regularly. They are both role models for me for different reasons.

One seems to be able to do it all—she helps people in her job, she is great at being an adult even though she's still in her early 30s, she has a beautiful family and home, she takes care of herself. But she knows struggle too. And she tackles her struggles with the same focus, positivity, and directness with which she faces everything else. She reminds me of how capable I really am. The other friend has faced serious struggles as well, but she has never let that stop her from moving forward, being herself, and pursuing her goals. She has this gift of being truly unique and genuinely talented. She taught me to be a rebel before I knew I was one. And she inspires me to keep moving forward like she has. Yes, I can call them anytime, but sometimes it's enough just to think about them and feel inspired and proud to know them. Find people you can look up to and be inspired by.

If you are a caretaker dealing with a friend-turned-jerk, I encourage you to use the same techniques but in a different way. Allow your loved one to feel her pain and give her space and encouragement to reflect. Be ready for deep issues to spring up from silly arguments. When you're depressed almost everything is an existential crisis. Let the conversation go where it needs to go as your loved one works through her layers of feelings. Also, research books, movies, etc. about inspirational stories of overcoming struggle and share these possible role models with your loved one. My dad gave me a great book he read about Abraham Lincoln and his struggles with melancholy throughout his life—and look what Lincoln did despite his own pain. So many inspirational, historical figures have struggled with depression. Most importantly, please don't run away even if your loved one lashes out. Unless you are facing abuse (in which case I strongly urge you to save yourself before you try to save your loved one), don't run away, but don't let yourself be a doormat. Vent to trustworthy friends who will support you and show you love. Stand up for yourself but stay available.

I want you to know that when you're a depressed jerk, depression is the problem, and pushing people away or lashing out is not the answer. Force yourself to step outside of your blinded self-loathing and see what is in control. Give yourself time to reflect on your actions and talk to someone about your real issues. Also, look outside of yourself for inspiration. Don't compare yourself to others—you are unique—but try to use some of their lessons, ideas, and methods to help you face your own issues. And remember that you are irreplaceable and one day your strength might inspire someone else to keep fighting.

4
Stolen Identity

SOMETIMES DEPRESSION IS TRIGGERED BY TRAUMA; FOR ME, THOUGH, DEPRESSION CAME OUT OF NOWHERE. I faced similar stresses as my peers or family members, but those stresses overwhelmed me. On February 3, 2000, I started a journal. Starting in the third sentence I write, "I am so lost. I don't know what to do with myself or who to be. I can't decide things for myself until I know who I am." Just over one year later I ended up in the hospital. The biggest thing that happened between the journal entry and my hospitalization was that I went to college. That's it. No one knew what was going on. No one—not even I—understood that I was depressed. But it happened. It was real. I changed dramatically. It is a real chemical imbalance in my brain that causes depression. I didn't do anything wrong; it's not a personal flaw, a sin, or pretend. It's an illness.

Today I was sitting in the waiting room of my counselor's office, and a person who I gathered was about to take part in a group counseling session said to his companion, "It's probably just going to be the same crap as the last two times." Man, that hit me. His coarseness. I don't know his situation or the full context of his comment, and I don't mean to judge. However, it really made me think about the fact that many people either think mental illness is crap or therapy is crap. No matter what triggered your depression, know that it's real. Know that something is happening with the chemicals in your brain. There isn't anything wrong with *you* even though something is going on in your brain.

Less than a month before my suicide attempt, on January 22, 2001, I wrote, "Where do I start because I am at the end? ... They won't let people be who they are ... I am not right." I thought I had found my identity and that I was bad. I thought the world couldn't accept me and so I wasn't right. Depression fooled me into thinking that I was my depression. It took complete control. It permeated everything about me. Physically I was neglectful, emotionally I was wrecked, mentally I was burdened, and spiritually I was lost. I completely believed the lies my brain was telling me.

I don't know the finer details of the science of depression, but there is so much evidence to support the reality of mental illness—it's just a Google search away. It's real and you should believe it. And it takes complete healing. It can't be ignored or simply prayed away. It takes effort and possibly medication. It takes therapy and practice. And it takes time. Don't believe the lies your brain tells you, but also don't believe the naysayers. Depression is not a fiction. Therapy is not junk. Depression will steal your identity but therapy can help you find it again.

5

What about Your Friends?

I'M NOT GOING TO LIE TO YOU—YOU MAY LOSE SOME FRIENDS DUE TO DEPRESSION. Sometimes it's because you're a jerk, sometimes it's because they're jerks. But you may also very well have friends who stick close and pick up the slack. Don't shut out these friends. They want to help you, and they can help you just by loving you and being with you. Even in darkness relationships can grow if you allow your friends to nourish you. Your friends will respond to your depression in a variety of ways, but I want to talk about three: when you are rejected, when you are estranged, and when you are accepted.

When You Are Rejected

My family kept me pretty sheltered after my initial breakdown, but there was gossip and rejection. One dear friend questioned the reality of my struggle and the time I spent on recovering rather than working or going to school. (This was just a few months after my suicide attempt.) I was angry, and I decided I didn't need him in my life at that point. And I was right. He was not helping my recovery. However, a couple of years later he contacted me and revealed that he was experiencing his own mental health struggles and wanted to meet for advice or insight or just to talk. We ended up having a wonderful conversation and rekindled our friendship. When someone rejects you because of your illness, let them go but realize that their motivation could be anything. Maybe they are ignorant, maybe they are self-centered, maybe they are hateful, or maybe they are hurting. Maybe they need to see your pain before they can face their own. Maybe they reject you because they can't accept themselves. You may never know. Many people will not understand. Some friends may reject you. Just let them go. They are wrong. You have a real illness, and you need help. You don't need rejection so move on. If these friends come back, then you can decide whether you want them in your life, but when facing rejection just move along from the negativity.

When You Are Estranged

When I began college I spent a lot of time with my best

friend at the time. We were very close, and our friendship was very happy and supportive. We could laugh (a lot) together and talk deeply about life and ourselves. We shared our dreams and fears with each other. She is one of the closest friends I have ever had, but depression changed me. I began to withdraw from her as well as everything else. She had the misfortune of being forced into a front row seat for my deterioration and self-destruction. She tried to help me, she continued to show me love, but I became dark and secretive, paranoid, and obsessive. My depression had not yet been identified, and without medical intervention—which no one knew I needed—I spiraled and became a different person altogether. I was unable to be a friend at all. I was afraid of everything, detached from reality, and actually desperate to continue swimming in darkness. I didn't want real help. I believed I was becoming my true self. I was delusional. As difficult as it is for me to say, our friendship never fully recovered from the trauma my depression caused. There wasn't necessarily love lost—we were true friends—but there was pain. There was the reminder of the trauma we separately experienced. Depression causes pain for you and those who love you, and it may cause distance or estrangement. This happens in all kinds of relationships—depressed or not. This is just one of those things. You are not to blame because you are not your illness, but a hurt friend is not to blame either. Everyone has feelings. If you are a friend, of course please stick around, but if you can't, please know that your depressed friend is sick and needs support and medical help. Ask a mutual friend to step in, keep praying, or contact a medical professional if necessary, and also take care of yourself.

Dealing with mental illness can be traumatizing.

When You Are Accepted

The vast majority of my friends have been able to choose to accept me even when I am depressed. (Estranged friends may still accept you from a distance, of course.) I mentioned my two childhood friends in an earlier post. They have never once stopped loving, supporting, and accepting me. There are so many more like them, but I want to focus on two. When I lived in Oklahoma, I met a couple who warmly accepted me into their home and friend group. I began going to their house twice a week for social gatherings, and then I also began going over for sports games, dinner, or just to visit. During my third depressive episode I started going over there practically every day for hours at a time. They fed me, comforted me, let me cry, and made me laugh. I was so afraid to be alone, and they accepted that about me and allowed me to spend as much time as I wanted in their home. They talked to me, encouraged me, and listened to me. They gave so much of themselves—more than any friend must give—and treated me like family. You will find, as you struggle, that there are amazing people in this world strong enough and willing to love, support, and accept you. You may never know the lengths that someone will go for you until you need help. Reach out to your friends—some won't stick around, some won't be able to, but others will go above and beyond what you think you deserve. And I beg you to accept the love and support of your friends. Don't push away or pull away from a friend who is reaching out. They can very likely help you and maybe even save you.

6
Anxiety, My Old Friend

I DON'T REALLY LIKE TALKING ABOUT ANXIETY. I like to ignore it because it doesn't affect me the way it used to. I truly believe, in my case, anxiety has been easier to conquer than depression. Anxiety really can be controlled through behavioral therapy. By addressing your anxious triggers, practicing exposure therapy, and avoiding high-stress situations, you can try to live more normally. I believe this, and there is medical research to support this. In most cases, you don't have to be a slave to anxiety.

But before I talk about what you can do, I want to review the extremes to which my anxiety and phobias have taken me. This won't be pretty. Maybe I should start with the nights I barricaded myself in my apartment using furniture to block the front door for fear of rape or murder. There are the months where I constantly thought my fiancé, living several states away, was going to die, and I called him multiple times a day to check on him. There is when I stopped driving for fear of having a panic attack or a wreck. Or when I was afraid to go anywhere by myself, even the grocery store. And of course there is the agoraphobia—the intense fear of crowds—which caused severe panic attacks where I recklessly ran away to hide and weep in closets or bathroom stalls.. I've had daily, generalized anxiety and lived in isolation driven by fear. Living with anxiety closes down your life. It shuts you inside of yourself with fear guarding the door. It takes over your brain and forces you to consider all the bad possibilities. It sucks away your ability to experience joy for fear of experiencing anxiety.

Anxiety is a major depressive trigger for me now. When I feel anxious or fearful it quickly grows into something bigger. So I think I'll start with the Umpqua Community College (UCC) mass shooting in Roseburg, Oregon. The morning after the tragedy, I became fearful for my family, anxious about letting them go to school and work for fear of a sick person with a gun. At first this seemed like a normal response. But I began crying when my husband was leaving for work. I cried for an hour feeling like something was bound to happen in this crazy world. I called my mother. She talked me down enough to take my daughter to school. But I began crying again once I got back to my car. I kept crying for several more hours but not about the shooting. The single kernel of anxiety planted by the coverage I read of the shooting grew. I began to fear for our nation and our world. I began to fear that we were completely broken and could never get any better. Then somewhere along the line my horror at the brokenness of the world turned into hatred of my own brokenness. I felt unable to help the world, which made me think how incapable I am generally, which made me begin to think about specific things that I can't do, which made me ruminate on the things I don't but should do, which made me think about how horrible I am, which made me think I am worthless, which made me feel like a burden, which made me think maybe I should do the world a favor and disappear. And then I went through that process over and over and over again, always leading back to distraught self-loathing. Although this shooting probably caused anxiety in many people, I lost control, not about the politics (although I have opinions concerning guns and the US), but about the fear of death or loss. And I hadn't fully recovered more than a week later. My nerves were shaky, my body stayed tense; I was more jumpy.

For me, anxiety triggers negative thought patterns—neural pathways deeply grooved from overuse—they're easy to find and easy to travel. My brain gets stuck traveling these pathways over and over, often leading to flickers of suicidal ideation. This is a difficult part of my fight—shielding myself from triggers. I can't read as much news as I want; I practically never watch news stories. (Watching the Ferguson grand jury decision announcement and aftermath sent me into a tailspin as well.) I mostly stopped watching *CSI* and *Law and Order*. I don't often go to places where there will be large crowds of people. I avoid my triggers as best I can. But there are other things that I had to face and get over. Driving, for instance. I hate to drive, but it isn't practical in my particular situation to completely avoid driving. It has taken me a couple of years of effort to feel semi-comfortable driving on the freeway. Even today, I had the irrational fear that if I turned my stiff neck too quickly it would lock up, causing me to be unable to look over my shoulder making me surely have a wreck. Ridiculous! What was the point of that thought? But I had it, and my heart rate began to rise; however, I began to rationalize with myself immediately, and I came up with a plan just in case it did happen. All positive thinking. And then I was able to let it go.

This simple method probably seems impossible to some of you, but I have been aggressively working on fighting my anxiety since 2007. I have been meditating regularly (at least four times a week) for six years. I began using exposure therapy to overcome anxieties that I could not live with. I have done a dialectical behavioral skills class. I still receive counseling to fight negative self-talk. Fighting anxiety takes a ton of work, specifically some kind of behavioral therapy. Depression will swallow you whole; anxiety will choke the life out of you. So don't go down without a fight. Find therapy to help you fight your anxiety. You don't have to live with it. I used to suffer terrible panic attacks; they are mostly gone because now I can usually slow down my anxiety and center myself. I used to be agoraphobic and couldn't help but panic and weep when surrounded by a crowd. Now, if I must go somewhere crowded, I may be uncomfortable, but I don't lose control.

Of course, it's not gone. When I face a real tragedy, like

the UCC shooting at the community college in Oregon, I often unintentionally overreact. It takes a toll, and it can take days to recover, but only days—not weeks or months. I grocery shop alone, I drive on the freeway, I even go to the occasional crowded concert. All of these things would have been problems for me at different points in my life, but I am recovering. If you need a place to get started, I strongly recommend *The Anxiety and Phobia Workbook* by Edmund J. Bourne. I wish I could buy you all copies. Please, please pick up this book and read it if you suffer from anxiety of any kind. You can get better if you are willing to work at it and know that recovery takes time and commitment. Please don't give in to your anxiety. Seek professional help or start with a good self-help book, but don't give up. You can get your life back from the stranglehold of anxiety.

7

Trying to Find Pleasure When You Feel Nothing but Pain

6:30am Another day of defeat. Exhaustion has led me to detached sadness. The negative thoughts in my brain seem so loud against my tired silence. I talk a lot about fighting back, but I often fail miserably. Lately, I look at food and just move on, put off by the work of fixing or just eating it, not even enjoying what I make for my family. I never exercise beyond dancing in my kitchen while I clean. There is so much research about the tremendous benefits of exercise for depression. My home. It's still messy and I feel overwhelmed. Dishes make me feel like crying. Strike that—actually crying. I can hear some of you now, "You had dirty dishes last week." Yep. I've lost control of my home. And I let my daughter see and live in this mess. I let my husband experience the chaos left behind by my neglect. Worthless.

7:30am Sitting outside with music on the headphones helped. A little hip-hop bravado gave me some confidence. I can do some stuff. I'm still writing if nothing else. No more tears, anyway. My darkness began to part about eight songs in. Now there's a little light. I can move forward.

8:00am So do I turn this into something about how I struggle with keeping my life balanced or about what I do to shake the blues and boredom of depression? This morning I was sure today would be hard—maybe it will be, but I no longer feel worthless. Maybe one of my best skills, also one of my greatest luxuries, is my ability to build in time to snap a pattern of negativity. I get up at least six days a week an hour before my daughter. I never know what the morning will hold. So if I need to cry, I can do it before she wakes up. If I'm feeling good I can enjoy myself for an hour before I have to do any work. I take time for myself to feel good after every task or set of tasks. I watch an episode of TV or Ellen on YouTube, listen to music, snuggle with my pets (one dog and two cats!), or sit on my back porch. I read the Bible or quotes I've underlined in my favorite books. Some things will keep me happy for a time, so I keep coming back to them until they no longer make me happy. Some things bring me happiness for a few days, some for a few years. I have watched so much Star Trek (*TNG* and *Voyager*) over the past five-plus years, but it still makes me happy. The good guys are compassionate and progressive, and they always win. I like to listen to Kanye West. He's kind of crazy, but what do I care? His music makes me feel good. It's a little serotonin burst.

9:00am Got my daughter off to school. Back on the back porch with coffee and music on headphones again (Queen B). The sun came out and I can see blue sky between the white clouds. It's still only nine. I have time.

9:30am I like being with friends; it feels nice to take my mind off of myself. But I love being alone. That is when I work on retraining my brain to experience pleasure. After a while, depression sucks the joy out of everything. When you used to laugh there is sorrow. When you used to care there is emptiness. It's gnawing. It makes you even more raw. I have watched *The Office* weeping at my inability to laugh. I have grown angry at my inability to enjoy making art. I have given up on my ability to finish a book. I have sat in silence for hours because any stimulation reminds me of my everlasting despair.

Don't neglect your ability to experience pleasure. Keep going back to anything that has given you harmless comfort (don't do hard drugs or self-harm). So you like something childish, square, or weird; it's far better to be happy than cool. I'm a 34-year-old white woman, but when I'm alone I lip-sync Jay Z with gusto. I'm a Trekkie, I've been known to jam to Taylor Swift and Miley Cyrus, I read *Twilight*, I've watched *Supernatural* an ungodly amount of times. I'm not going to waste my precious energy feeling ashamed about what makes me happy when I am trying to save my own life.

Keep spending time with your partner and friends. Work through your indifference because it just might make you feel better. My husband and I have at-home date night twice a week every week. I get to plan one date a week, he gets to plan the other. We prioritize spending time together to find pleasure. We play board games, listen to music, read poetry, or just talk. But we schedule time to find pleasure together.

Keep trying new things. So you once liked TV but haven't enjoyed it in months. Binge a bunch of new shows just in case one interests you. I watched *Sons of Anarchy* this summer for the first time and found myself more engaged in TV than I had been in a long time. I started a free trial for a music streaming service on a whim a few months ago. It has kind of transformed my life (definitely worth my money). I listen to so much more music than I used to. I splurged on a refurbished pair of nice headphones. Instant pleasure most of the time. That might change one day, but I'm going to enjoy it as long as I can. One day at a time.

Keep feeding your brain positivity. I used to douse my brain in media that mirrored my depression. I fed myself messages of isolation and sadness. Movies, music, and books about the meaninglessness of suffering, and the depths of human despair. At first it made me feel like I wasn't alone. I felt connected. But when you feel lonely and you keep hearing someone talk about loneliness, you start to feel your own loneliness more deeply. The escape begins to reflect your own life too closely. Try putting some positive messages in your mind too. It won't be easy. I really like the song "The Man" by Aloe Blacc. I liked it from the start. My dad used to tell me "You the girl," so it brought back happy memories of encouragement. However, when I began to push myself to sing along I got a lump in my throat. Trying to actually say genuinely, "Go ahead and tell everybody I'm the man," was too tough. I sang along with tears and disbelief, but I kept singing. And I kept listening to the song every day. And it got easier to sing along. All last year I kept telling myself, "I'm the man." It didn't matter how true it was. I could feel it even if only for tiny moments. Practice positivity, practice events that give you pleasure even when they don't. You might be surprised to find yourself smiling one day.

10:30am I've been listening to music and writing for an hour. I feel all right. My house is still a wreck. I haven't exercised. But I found a little pleasure. I put my plan to work (beat back negativity with music and writing), and now I feel like I don't have to go back to bed. It took most of the morning, but things are better than four hours ago. If you can't find pleasure no matter how hard you try, which happens sometimes, know that it is temporary. If you work hard on therapy, keep feeding your brain positivity no matter how painful it is, keep trying, you can come out on the other side. It just takes time and effort. Whatever effort you can give—even if it's just getting out of bed—do it. Keep practicing life. One day you'll feel things again besides pain. If you don't have anyone helping you, find help. Friends, family, counselors, hotlines—find someone and tell them how empty you are. You can be happy again. I can be happy again. And for now, I'm keeping the music on just in case.

8
Talking to Myself

THIS MORNING, WHEN I GOT BACK TO MY CAR AFTER DROPPING MY DAUGHTER OFF AT SCHOOL, MY CAR WOULDN'T START. Seriously. I tried six times to start it with no luck. So I called my husband at home. We only have one car, and the school is only three-quarters of a mile from our house, so he started walking to the school. I was angry, so rather than sit and wait for him, I decided to walk home to get some energy out.

As I walked I kept repeating in my head, "I hate my life." Overdramatic negative self-talk. But about halfway home I realized that my rhythmic repeating "I hate my life" had turned into the rhythmically similar hook of the Kendrick Lamar song "i," which says, "I love myself." I have been listening to that song a lot lately, so it was fresh on my mind and somewhere along the line positivity took over in my brain. The rhythm of my pace and thoughts triggered another thought, and because I have been trying to fill my brain with positive music the thought that came back was "I love myself."

Negative self-talk is brutal, and everyone does it sometimes. But when you're depressed you get stuck in a feedback loop. One negative comment to yourself can cause hours of repetitive internal negativity. I've been compiling some of my most-negative thoughts as part of a homework project from my counselor; here are a few excerpts that I wrote down during a moment of deep despair: "I can't keep going, I am alone," "I have little (if any) monetary value," "I don't want to keep going," "There is no escape," "It is all too much," "I am a bad parent," "I can't help my husband enough," "I can't bring myself to leave the house," "Nothing can help me." It goes on and on in the same vein. Doubt and self-loathing. The project I'm doing is to come up with three positive thoughts to counter each negative one. Then I have to practice reading the positive thoughts three times a day.

For instance, for the thought "I can't do this," I could say these three things: 1. I have already successfully done this before through more difficult circumstances. 2. I don't have to fight alone; people are reaching out to me and showing support because they care about me. 3. Isaiah 40:29 "[God] gives strength to the weary and increases the power of the weak." Since I choose to rely on faith in God to give me meaning despite my suffering, I like using Bible verses as positive thoughts to counter negative feelings. Quotes and song lyrics could work as well. Besides stuffing your brain with positive thoughts, the key to fighting negative self-talk is to stop it as soon as you can. The more you ruminate and the longer you wait, the harder it will be to stop.

Let's say your brain is a neighborhood, and the different parts of your brain are the houses. Think of yourself alone inside one of the houses where your depression resides (amygdala, thalamus, and hippocampus): when it catches fire, you're going to immediately run to an exit, right? That's the healthy response. Negative self-talk is the fire, and the healthy response is to run away from it before you lose your chance to escape and are consumed by the fire. Try to run to another part of your brain that isn't as deeply under the control of your depression, such as the prefrontal cortex where you can try to regain control of the situation.

Don't wait to see whether the fire will go out on its own; if you are depressed, it won't, so try not to ruminate. This takes time and effort (again, it always takes time and effort), but if you practice, sometimes you will be able save yourself just by running to another part of your brain for help.

Also, as this example hopefully illustrates, it can be therapeutic to learn about how the depressed brain works. (I have only a super-simplistic understanding.) For me, visualizing the action physically happening in my brain makes me feel less crazy. If I can understand the differences between how my brain works and how a healthy brain works, I feel more in control. The knowledge makes me feel more prepared to fight because I feel like I better know my enemy.

I waste a lot of time on negative self-talk and tell myself

I can't help it; I can't control it. But I am not totally helpless. Some days it will be too much and I will lose the battle, but most days I can exert some control over my thinking because I have been practicing for so long. Therapy has given me tools and skills to fight. If you are depressed, find a therapist to teach you these skills and to explain to you the way your brain works. Remember that you are unique and valuable and you deserve help. You don't deserve to hear the negative things you tell yourself, so learn how to stop giving in to negative rumination. Retrain your brain to fight back against negative self-talk. And be gentle with yourself. Love yourself. Truly believe that you are worthy of healing. Speak nicely to yourself—you deserve it.

9
Crying Out to God

I HAVEN'T ATTENDED CHURCH REGULARLY SINCE 2000. After my initial breakdown, church made me too emotional. For a few years, any time I would try to attend a service, I would have to leave because I would begin weeping. There really was, for a time, something about church that I could not handle. I also began questioning my Christian faith during and throughout my first two depressive episodes. Finally, I fully stepped away from my faith in about 2006 and began calling myself agnostic. I was agnostic until I returned to Christianity in 2012, but I didn't return to a church. Church didn't interest me; my liberal political values seemed to make me an outsider. And the music is still too much, emotionally, for me to handle.

All of this is still true, but as I got deeper into my personal relationship with God, I really felt compelled to commune with other Christians. Last month I started attending a weeknight small group meeting for a church here in Tacoma. To be honest, it has been great. The people are genuine and welcoming. I don't have to worry about crowds or emotional music, but we pray together and discuss the Bible. And I feel blessed. I'm a little awkward with new people, true, but the benefits far outweigh my social discomforts.

What I really want to address, though, is why I came back to the faith I grew up with. I spent the first 18 years of my life growing up closely aligned with the Protestant church. It was a huge and wonderful part of my life, but my blind acceptance made my faith weak. As I became depressed I became consumed with spiritual doubt and resentment. I needed to step away, but by 2012, I was desperate. Before I picked up a Bible or reached out for prayer, I began crying out to God in my despair. I was consumed with suicidal ideation; every tool was a weapon, every landscape was a potential location. In anguish I asked aloud for divine intervention; I didn't know what else to do. I was so lost, so dark, so deeply alone. I had to believe that something could save me, and I was convinced that no person was strong enough. Without belief in God, I was going to kill myself.

So I began calling out—talking to God. I was sad and angry. I had nothing nice to say to Him really. No worship, no thankfulness, just pain and suffering. But it eventually gave me just enough strength to call my parents and tell them I desperately needed help. And, as usual, they gave it unconditionally. My sister found me an amazing Christian counselor who deftly guided me through my recovery. She helped me heal and spiritually nurtured me by teaching me spiritual self-acceptance through God's unconditional love for me.

But why Christianity? It began as a decision based on authenticity, to be honest. I'm a white woman from the southern United States brought up in Protestantism. I thought, politically, it was the most authentic place to start my return to spirituality. It sounds lame and unromantic, but it's the truth. What is also the truth though is that once I really began to study the Bible and Jesus and talk to God regularly, I didn't feel the need for anything more. Christianity has satisfied my spirit. I have found hope and healing. I still struggle with doctrine, I'm not a literalist; I'm still liberal and a feminist, and I still like to keep my spirituality close to my chest. I'm still learning, but I am spiritually happy. Developing and nurturing my spiritual self has helped me heal and maintain mental health.

I want to briefly look at a couple of verses that have helped me through depression. First, Romans 12:2: "Do not conform to the pattern of this world, but be transformed by the renewing of your mind. Then you will be able to test and approve what God's will is—his good, pleasing and perfect will." In 2013 I felt completely lost in my life. Unsure about everything. And I was mentally exhausted by my depression. To think that I could be transformed and renewed by my faith and communion with God was strengthening. And having hope that God would restore my clarity was invigorating. I believed I could get better, and I did.

The second verse is from *The Message* version of the Bible. First Peter 5:6: "So be content with who you are, and don't put on airs. God's strong hand is on you; he'll promote you at the right time. Live carefree before God; he is most careful with you." As I continued to struggle with healing I felt spiritually new but otherwise lost. I felt I didn't fit in with Christians. My spirituality had only slightly changed my political values, so outside of theological discussion, I felt detached from other, more conservative Christians. I get along with intellectuals and artists who often don't believe in Jesus' divinity. This verse reminds me that I can only be what God made me to be, and I should love myself because I am His creation. He will take care of me, and guide me at the right times, so I shouldn't worry. God convicted me to attend church, and gave me a personal connection to a member of a good church. I haven't had to search for a church; I like the one He led me to. I like the people, and I feel accepted as a fellow believer.

As I continue to struggle, I plan to hold tightly to my faith. It has been a blessing to me for the past three years, and I still cry out to God on my bad days. And I think He gives me strength and guidance. And above all, He gives me purpose in my pain, and meaning in my suffering. Jesus suffered immensely, so He knows my pain. God has a plan for my life, so everything that happens has meaning and is molding me to be what He desires. I choose to believe, and that choice has made quite a difference in my life.

10

For My Daughter

I keep thinking I can't do this to my family. I can't make them go through this again. Any of them. I'm trying to be open and honest, but it's hard to show them how I'm really feeling. I don't want them to worry. I don't want them to suffer, but they do. They can't help it because they love me, but I hate putting them through this torture. I love them so much. I don't want to cause anyone pain. I feel enough pain for all of you. I don't want you to suffer with me. I want to shield you. But it's too much to keep inside. It will kill me to keep it inside.

I wrote that a couple of days ago during my darkest moment of a bad day. I was hurting and afraid. Already I can see the stress my family is feeling. They're concerned. But it is better for me to be open than let the depression fester under a balanced facade. However, it is awful watching my illness hurt my loved ones. I feel like a really terrible person. And I'm afraid that I can't stop hurting them unless I stop living. It's gut-wrenching.

In 1941 one of my all-time, top five, favorite authors—Virginia Woolf—killed herself after a lifelong struggle with chronic depression. Woolf was a beautiful, astonishing writer, and her suffering and eventual suicide bothers me. I feel heartbroken for the pain she felt, mainly because I feel like I understand at least a little of what she suffered. Her portrayals of mental illness in her work are breathtakingly honest while also almost lyrical or poetic. Even her suicide note (which is widely available through a web search) is beautifully heartbreaking. It speaks so deeply to me because I have been in a similar mental space.

But I have something in my family that Woolf did not have—a child. When I think about causing pain to my family, I feel that the pain I cause now is greater than any pain suicide would cause. (This is a depression lie.) With one exception. I can't deny the blaring fact that my suicide would cause infinitely more pain to my daughter than anything I am doing now.

A generous friend told me recently that nothing can replace a mother, and I believe her. We are all irreplaceable, but if you have a good relationship with your mother, then she probably seems even more irreplaceable than most others. My mother is incredibly important to me. I could go on and on (and on and on) about her love, wisdom, grace, humility, loyalty, bravery, endurance, commitment, and patience. She is my hero. She's not perfect, but perfect is boring—she's better than perfect. What would I have done without her? What if she had checked out when I was a child? I would be a completely different person.

So what would my daughter do without me? She loves me so much, she shows so much affection, we laugh and talk, I comfort her when she's hurt or sad. I have been with her almost every single day of her life. Why would I ever leave her? Why would I cause such massive devastation in her life? I wouldn't and I won't. But I can't completely shield her from my illness. When it takes over I cannot hide it. She was three and four years old during my last episode, and so she does remember some of it. In fact, I believe her first memories are from that time, when she and I moved where my parents live for four months so I could recover. She remembers that I was sad a lot and cried a lot. I tell her that I have a disease that makes me sad. She accepts that, and she accepts that my disease is real and not just regular sadness. How she seemingly understands that, I don't know. But she supports me as best she can, with hugs or tissues. I try not to cry in front of her, and I never weep in front of her. I don't want her to see me lose control. But I can't hide the lethargy, the messy house, the unwashed hair, the puffy red eyes. If I continue to get worse, she will eventually know that I'm sick again.

Despite all of that, she gives me strength. She gives me my biggest reason to keep going. And it doesn't just stop at being her mom. This disease can be passed down genetically. She may face depression one day, and I have to be there to help her—like my mom has been there for me. I have to. I don't want her to give up. Ever. I want her to live a long, happy life, knowing who she is and that she is loved immensely and unconditionally. I can't let her down. I don't want to let any of my loved ones down, but if I'm being honest, I feel a greater responsibility to her. Even if I was a burden to my family (I am not), I am still important to my loving daughter. Virginia Woolf may be one of my favorite authors, but I won't follow in her footsteps. My family needs me. My family wants me. And I want to be here for my family. For my daughter.

11
Standing Up to Stigma

IF YOU CAN BELIEVE IT, I USED TO KEEP MY STRUGGLES WITH DEPRESSION SECRET. At first I only shared with people who had proven their loyalty to me. People I felt I could trust. I was ashamed of my weakness. I knew it was a disease, but it felt like a flaw. And my suicide attempt was even more of a secret. I was afraid that people would stop trusting me and feel unsafe around me. I was afraid of rejection.

Until I was diagnosed, I had no idea what was happening.

I felt like I was somehow transforming into something greater but ultimately doomed. My family thought I was extremely moody and sensitive. But when I finally broke down and was then diagnosed, we had a scary name to put on my self-destruction. I mentioned before that my parents shielded me from most of the reactions to what little information of the situation leaked out. There was gossip and criticism, I'm sure, but all I saw were the flower arrangements and encouraging cards. But I know people were talking—my friends, my parents' friends. I heard enough to know that not everyone was sending well-wishes. Maybe the biggest kick I got was when my new sorority asked for all their stuff back just a couple of weeks after my suicide attempt in a short, terse card. Of course, I also received a beautiful card from my New Testament professor as well. It was always a mix of love and rejection. It always has been.

In every episode, people walk away and people come closer. I had a good friend from high school who stayed very loyal to me upon my initial breakdown. He went to a different college, where the news had reached my other friends who went to that school, and he told me that he refused to listen to anyone's telling of my story—he waited until he could hear it from me. He stood up for me by shunning the gossip. At the second college I went to, where I ultimately graduated, I noticed on my first day of class a girl from my high school. I was a little exasperated. I thought surely she had heard the gossip about me. Later in the semester we were put in a small group together, and despite my fears, she was really friendly. This was the start of what became and still is a beautiful friendship. She had heard nothing about me really, and I had heard none of the gossip about her having her daughter when she was 19. We were both afraid of what the other had heard about us, and this gave us a commonality to build a close relationship. We accepted each other's "issues" without question.

But it is more than just gossip; it's a systemic problem too. In 2005 I started graduate school. My first two years I maintained a 4.0 GPA, but at the beginning of my third year in a three-year program I became severely depressed again (third episode) and was unable to concentrate on anything but trying to stay afloat. I took incompletes for most of my classes that year and ended up leaving school without officially withdrawing—it was too depressing—or getting a degree. One year later I felt much better and wanted to reenroll and finish my degree. My former professors were very supportive, but I did have to provide a letter from my psychiatrist vouching that I was no longer crazy. I felt a bit embarrassed, but I did it, and I was readmitted, but again failed to finish my degree due to my fourth episode.

I thought about going back to graduate school last year too. I even met with an advisor and had my transcripts sent in. But because of my grades in my last two years of graduate school, they asked for a copy of my medical records or letters from my doctors from the time to prove I had been ill. Ouch. My medical records? Maybe cancer patients have to go through the same hoops—I honestly don't know, but it felt pretty terrible, like I needed a co-lender on a mortgage, but the mortgage was on my sanity. How have I faced this reaction? I gave in and then I gave up. I didn't return to school and I feel discouraged by the hoops I will seemingly have to jump through anywhere to return to school. It is painful to me. I feel like a failure who can't try again without proof that I'm not crazy. Then it makes me think that I'm not good enough anyway; I'm too damaged for any graduate program. I don't have the chops. I give in to the depression when I think about it. I feel flawed instead of ill. I feel worthless rather than chemically unbalanced.

Google defines *stigma* as "a mark of disgrace associated with a particular circumstance, quality, or person." I'm sure it sounds familiar to many of you who are depressed. We stigmatize ourselves, are stigmatized by people, and even feel systemic stigma. No one wants you to wear a red D on your chest, but they treat you as if there is one there anyway. Don't be discouraged, though, and don't be silent. If you need to speak about your mental illness in order to heal, like I have, then do it despite the possible rejection. Your healing is more important than the stigma you may face. If you choose to hide your depression, know that your fear of stigma is real but it is a systemic, societal problem—there is nothing wrong with *you*. You have an illness.

One of the reasons my family couldn't save me before my suicide attempt was their lack of understanding of what was going on due to the fact that they had never really spent time with an openly depressed person. I want to speak up so that others can more quickly recognize what they are facing and maybe save themselves and so that families can save their loved ones. I speak out despite the stigma because I want to save lives, and stigma is one of the things killing severely depressed people.

Knowing and meeting acceptance as well as facing rejection has given me the courage to speak up. It isn't too hard to hide mild depression, especially if it is a single episode, but when you face it every one or two years for more than a decade, it will eat you alive if you keep silent. I'm not telling you to shout it from the rooftop (unless you want to), but I feel better when I am completely open. I don't give the kind of details over a coffee date as I do here, but if I hid my depression I would be forced to hide half of my adult life. I couldn't talk about how I've become the person I am, how I met the people I've met, or how I came to live where and how I live. I am a chronic depressive; knowing and accepting that comes with the territory of being my friend. It doesn't mean you have to sit with me when I cry, but it does mean you have to accept me as I am.

12

On Suicidal Ideation

By 2001 I had spent more than a year toying with the meaninglessness of my existence and a desire for an end to the pain I felt. I didn't plan how to kill myself, though. I didn't let the thoughts become more than vague desires. But when I mentally broke down, suicide came to me as an epiphany would. The moment is still so scarily clear in my memory. I sat in a girlfriend's dorm room crying and distraught when the thought came to me like light in the darkness—"It's time to kill yourself." I took that thought as truth, and I abruptly left my girlfriend's room and went to the bathroom. I stood looking in the mirror extremely afraid. Part of me didn't want to do it, but I felt I had to—it seemed the best if not the only solution to my pain. So I returned to my dorm room and began taking all of the over-the-counter medicine I had—Nyquil and extra-strength Tylenol PM—and after talking to my mother and boyfriend, telling neither anything about what I was doing but unable to hide my distress, I fell asleep.

I talk pretty openly here about the fact that I have suicidal thoughts when I am at the mercy of my depression. The technical term is suicidal ideation. My suicidal thoughts begin as fleeting, but if I allow myself to ruminate on them they will develop. I've talked about the grooved neural pathways in my brain before. The more I think certain thoughts the easier it is to think those again in the future. Every time I walk down a path I make it more walkable for myself later. In 15 years I've done a lot of suicidal ideation—often it is as simple as "I wish I could just sleep away the rest of my life"—but it can develop into practicing parts of a plan or actually giving in.

For me, suicidal ideation came and went with my depressive episodes, but mostly it remained fleeting thoughts until 2012. At that time the suicidal thoughts grew in my isolation. I felt increasingly worthless and burdensome. Again, suicide seemed the best choice to free myself and my loved ones from my pain. I had a location and method planned. I was in the early stages of practicing my method when I knew I could not do it. But I also knew I might not be able to stop myself without help. Again, I was at the mercy of suicidal thoughts. I finally called my sister in tears and asked for help. She has always taken my depression very seriously; she has never refused to do anything I ask for my health, and even has done more than I have asked. I used all of the little self-control I had left and called her—and that saved my life. It was the turning point where I let go of my plan. I had a long struggle and recovery in front of me, but I haven't been nearly that close to suicide since that time.

If you think about suicide in any form, know that those thoughts are lies of an ill brain. In most cases, healthy brains want to survive. Even if you don't want to die but you wish you weren't alive, you are playing a risky game. If you feed suicidal ideation, it will grow. It grew in me to near-fatal proportions. Do not welcome those thoughts into your mind. In my case, they bang on the door yelling and screaming sometimes, but I fight hard to ignore them. I know that once I start, those thoughts may take control and cause me to make tragic decisions. Any moment that you can find the strength to tell someone how deeply you're in the pit, do it. Most people will immediately drop everything to help save your life. If you encounter someone who won't help you, tell someone else. Don't stop asking for help if you need it. Call the suicide prevention hotline—1-800-273-8255—or your physician. Don't believe the lies your brain is telling you because they are just that—lies.

Miraculously, after I drank all my Nyquil and took all of my Tylenol in 2001, I woke up to the sound of my phone ringing. Two hours after I fell asleep, my parents had arrived based on my distraught phone call. I drunkenly made my way to the front of my dorm and emotionally broke down when I saw my parents. Still, I didn't tell them what I had done. I felt safer with them there and just wanted to forget it; I no longer wanted to die. But within 15 minutes I began vomiting, and at their pleas, I told them what I had done. My mother had made our family physician's office number easily accessible just in case she needed it for me, and they immediately called at this point.

My physician later told me that for many years he had spent his Wednesday afternoons out of the office doing community work. The day my parents called was only the second time in at least a decade that he had been in his office on a Wednesday afternoon. Miraculously—again—he personally answered the office phone and told my parents to immediately take me to the emergency room. Over the next 48 hours, I had multiple doctors tell me that I had certainly done a thorough job and that if I had not immediately received treatment, I would have slowly died over the next week from liver failure.

My suicide attempt wasn't a cry for help—it was a near-fatal victory for my depression. My cry for help was when I called my parents. I continued to obey the command of my depression, but something inside of me—maybe my intense love for my parents—made me call them and just tell them something was wrong with me. And that call saved my life even though I thought nothing could save me.

You too can be saved. You just need to reach out to someone somewhere who can get you treatment. Make the tough call and say what you need to say. Every time I have suicidal thoughts beating down my door, I fight, and when I'm not strong enough on my own, I call someone. Sometimes I just need to hear a supportive voice, sometimes I need to be physically rescued. Be aware of what is happening in your brain. Resist suicidal ideation at all costs, and call someone and be honest. One moment of strength, one phone call can really save you. I know because it happened to me. And I'm still here and will always fight.

13
The Tragic Beauty of Depression

When I was 18, before I was diagnosed with depression, I felt lost and unsure of myself. I didn't know what I wanted out of life—I had little to no self-confidence, although I continued to publicly perform as if I was fine. When I was alone, I would be overwhelmed with insecurity about everything. I felt incapable, but I kept going through the motions, doing all the things an 18-year-old girl from my background should do.

By the time I turned 19, I began to lose my grip on reality. I began to believe that I was finally transforming into my true self when really I was just being consumed by disease. I felt that I was finally seeing the world clearly and it was just lies covered in false loveliness. I thought the pain I felt was a result of my clarity and most others were blind to the truth. I clung to this perception and thus to my depression. It felt painful but special. I was lost but inspired. I wrote poetry and short stories as well as journaling. I read books and listened to music that reflected my feelings. I daydreamed more than interacted. My soul felt full of tragic beauty. I felt wonderfully flawed. I thought my pain meant I felt life in a way others couldn't. I was part of a special few. I envisioned myself taking an unpaved but beautiful path through life as opposed to staying on the main road. It seemed so romantic to me.

I look back now and know my illness was conning me. It told me what I wanted to hear at first, but by the time I could no longer control it, it began telling me other things. I thought that perhaps I wasn't meant for this world; perhaps I could not survive among those blind to my "truth." I began to feel rejected by the world. I began to see myself as an outsider. It became harder to interact. I became paranoid about what others thought of me. No matter how special I was, I would never be accepted. I felt trapped. I felt there was nowhere to go. No one would ever accept me once they saw what I was. There was something terribly wrong with me.

Eventually depression began eating away at me, taking back whatever passion it had given me, and leaving me hollow and hopeless. It was a fluid transition; I never saw it coming until it was too late. I was too far in to pull myself out. The depressed parts of my brain took complete control of my whole body. The six weeks before my suicide attempt I lost 15 pounds and acquired a severe B12 deficiency because I stopped eating. I stopped communicating with anyone except the people I had met in online forums, skipping class and sorority functions. I slept in my clothes on top of my bed to avoid getting dressed or making my bed. Showers were painful because any sensation of touch reminded me of my physical existence. I couldn't focus on anything but my pain. Although I had once felt special, the self-loathing and neglect that replaced the passion were infinitely more powerful.

Even after I was diagnosed and told the severity of my medical condition, I was skeptical. I couldn't believe an illness could have changed my ability to see and experience reality. It had been so real. It was real, but I was being blinded to reality. I was in a dream created by my depression, and it became a nightmare. I know what it's like to want to stay depressed. I was initially somewhat resistant to treatment. But once it began (counseling three times a week), my counselor began explaining what depression is and what it feels like—a giant wet wool blanket smothering you and making it impossible to move, see light, or feel warmth. Then I began to believe. I was dumbfounded that others had felt what had seemed so singular to my experience. Depression had masked itself as something unique, but it plays the same tricks on millions around the world.

Even now my depression lies to me about taking my medicine or needing counseling. Depression doesn't want to be fixed. You may think you want to stay depressed, but that is your depression lying to you. It wants you and makes you believe you want or even need it. In my life, I must fight or my depression will win. I must be medicated and daily practice skills, sick or well. I must stay on alert and do my best to parse through my thoughts to determine what is true and what is a lie. It's a never-ending battle. I read books or journals that remind me of that tragic but seemingly beautiful few months when I was 18 to 19. They still look beautiful in my memory, but I know the darkness behind them now. I know the shell of a person I became. I say it a lot, but with severe depression your only options are to fight or drown. It's all I've known for the past 15 years. It's taken away my career plans, my plans to have more children, my ability to financially contribute, and more. But I keep fighting. Despite my depression, I have a college degree, a wonderful marriage, and an amazing daughter. It has tried to prevent me from having all of this, but those are battles I've won, and I intend to win the war. Never give up, never give in, and don't be fooled. Fight to win the real battle.

14

When I Started Reciting the Rosary

In the fall of 2008, I had just barely recovered from my third depressive episode, gotten married, and moved to Florida with my new husband when I found out I was pregnant. The pregnancy was unplanned, and my family in Texas was very concerned about how my brain would react to the hormonal changes in my body—and of course I had to get off my medication. Yes, we were poor and had no health insurance, and I was desperately looking for work while my husband was a PhD student studying and teaching, but I had always wanted to be a mother. I was excited about the pregnancy; my husband was scared. Everyone was concerned about me, but as my mother told me when I called to say I was pregnant, "Laura Grace, a baby is a blessing." Despite an extremely tight financial state at the time, I felt pretty good. I was mentally well throughout the pregnancy. I got back on an SSRI (selective serotonin reuptake inhibitor—the class of drugs most often prescribed to treat depression and anxiety) a week after the birth of my daughter, and I continued to do fairly well as a new mother. We moved back to Oklahoma so I could try to finish my graduate degree. I had a new daughter, was back in classes, and teaching again. I did it all for a few months—no postpartum depression at all, thank God!

However, something changed when I stopped breastfeeding. I lost all those new-mom hormones, and I was left with the same situation—new baby, classes, and teaching. It was too much. I faded out of my own classes and barely held on as a teacher, but I had to stay enrolled and continue teaching in order to keep the healthcare I desperately needed. I was again overwhelmed by sadness and anxiety; my brain was under such strain from the depression that I could not read, write, or discuss. I continued to be a devoted mother though, prioritizing my daughter. That is when I decided to try being a stay-at-home parent. I could do the parenting, but between that and trying to keep my own head above water, I was tapped.

The counselor I began seeing at the campus student health clinic while I was still enrolled really emphasized learning and practicing lifestyle skills as a way to control anxiety and depression along with medication and regular counseling. She immediately introduced me to the book *The Anxiety and Phobia Workbook*. It changed my life. It gave names to my anxious feelings and stories and strategies to combat my problems.

That is when I began meditating, among other things. I was unsure about how to meditate. I was agnostic at the time; I had no kind of spiritual meditative practices to fall back on, so I decided to just do something I liked. Although I grew up Protestant, I was, like many, attracted to the ritual of Catholicism. I thought the rosary was beautiful, really poetic. I loved the tangibility of counting beautiful beads and reciting romantic words. I mentioned my interest to my mother, and she contacted my Catholic aunt to see whether she had any advice. My aunt sent me a beautiful rosary and a book about praying the rosary. I thought, why not give it a try? I learned the words of the rosary quickly, and began silently saying it in a peaceful space daily. I really enjoyed it, although I didn't feel Zen or centered. I felt better though; it was nice making time to attempt to quiet my mind.

At times, I would say the rosary in moments of distress to calm myself down. This turned into a kind of prayer, I guess. I would desperately call out to Mary, who, in the tradition of the rosary, acts as a mediator. I would cry, "Holy Mary Mother of God, pray for us now and at the hour of our death!" I wasn't ready to return to God, but I was willing to take any help I could get—even from a mediator I didn't really know whether I believed existed. Again, it made me feel better, even though I was unsure whether I was meditating correctly, whether I was praying, whether there was any faith behind my words, or whether I was offensively using a religious practice that didn't belong to me. But I had read about the benefits of meditation, and the rosary had offered me a way in, so I took it.

I began saying the rosary at least once a day, rarely missing a day. I was committed. My anxiety didn't change dramatically, but I began to feel less depressed. As my depression lessened, I continued meditating. I struggled not to fall asleep; I tried noise-canceling headphones to get more focused. I tried lying down and sitting up—whatever it took to keep going. Two years in, I was hooked. I could use meditation in a pinch to often ward off panic attacks, and I took rosary beads with me everywhere I went. I even began making rosaries.

It has been six years now since I began saying the rosary. It hasn't kept me from getting depressed, but daily meditation for an extended period has dramatically changed my anxiety. I haven't taken Xanax in several years, and I have not had a panic attack in several years. I have put a lot of work into combating my anxiety—exposure therapy can be scary but incredibly useful—but I believe meditation has played a huge role in my improvement. It hasn't fixed me, but now I know how to center myself—get Zen. I don't wait until I need peace, I find peace daily whether or not I'm struggling. It now takes me ten to 15 minutes to really chill out. My body relaxes, my brain relaxes, and I get lost in a good way. My cares melt away for a little while. I have my body trained to relax on command, and it works. If I'm having a tough day with depression, meditation is hard, but I just keep trying.

I'm not saying I don't have limits any more. I still get depressed, I still struggle at parties, I still have to avoid tragic news stories, I've chosen not to have any more children, and

I still don't have a paying job, but I am so much more in control of myself than I was after my daughter was born. I'm also not saying you should start saying the rosary. You might find it ridiculous or blasphemous, and I may be appropriating something that doesn't belong to me. But I do encourage you to meditate somehow if you struggle with depression and anxiety. And give it a good try—20 minutes a few times a week for five years—before you tell yourself it won't work for you. So you fall asleep every time for a year—keep going. So you can't concentrate and get off track every time for two years—keep going. Every time you lose your place, don't give up, just pick it up at the last spot you remember. Commit to 20 minutes. You may struggle staying focused for months, but keep going. Try guided meditations, mindfulness, or more traditional forms of meditation. Try different things until you find something you like—spiritual or secular.

Living with chronic mental illness requires lifestyle accommodations. I have to limit my stress, take medicine, get rigidly regular sleep, practice skills to combat my phobias, and continually practice finding even momentary inner peace. Meditation is one of the most useful and valuable skills I have acquired. I'm a better partner, mother, and person when I daily center myself. This is not a quick fix though; it's part of a long-term plan to be used in addition to medical treatment and therapy. Fight every day, even if it's a 20-minute struggle trying to find peace. It slowly gets easier, based on my experience and mental heath research. Even the smallest tool can help you win the war.

15

I Love Myself!

I OFTEN GET COMMENTS ON MY BLOG AND FACEBOOK PAGE ABOUT HOW BRAVE I AM FOR FIGHTING MY ILLNESS AND WRITING SO OPENLY ABOUT IT. I do think of myself as a fighter, but brave? Firefighters are brave. To be honest, brave or not, I won't be quiet about it for the simple fact that I love myself. I won't be put in a corner. And because I love myself, I love you all too, and I believe you deserve to be heard too. I speak not so you'll listen, but so you'll feel strong enough to accept and love yourself and tell your story. And maybe that is brave in a world that doesn't want to hear our stories or expects us to suffer silently and alone.

Maybe I should be embarrassed and that's what is brave about it. I've admitted that I lose touch with reality sometimes and that my brain isn't normal. But my desire to break the socially expected silence that kills too many mentally ill people trumps my shame. I've done stupid stuff in the past that I'm ashamed of—some when I was depressed—but I'm not going to be ashamed of who I am.

In about 2003, when I was in college, I was in a Shakespeare class studying *King Lear* and furiously taking notes when my professor asked whether anyone had ever felt extreme existential anguish. Still looking at the notes I was writing, I raised my hand along with several others. The professor then asked whether anyone with their hand raised had ever experienced this kind of anguish for weeks at a time. Still busy writing notes, I didn't notice that I was the only one with my hand still up. Once I noticed the ensuing silence in the classroom, I looked up from my note-taking to find the professor looking at me skeptically, clearly making assumptions about me based on appearance and gossip.

He scoffed and said to me in front of the entire class, "You've lived a privileged life; you can't possibly understand what I'm talking about. Put your hand down." I sheepishly put my hand down, but I was embarrassed and angry. I was embarrassed that I had raised my hand at all and angry that my honesty had been rejected. I feared that my classmates thought either that I was crazy or that I was a fool and a liar. My professor's opinion was clear. I was being silenced by some person who didn't know me but judged me based on assumptions.

But depression doesn't care who you are, who your

family members are, the amount of money you have, or what you do with your life. We all meet different conflicts in our lives, so why does mental illness deserve especially rigid stigma?

But during that time, I also met several strong women who told me their depression stories. Their stories were memories of devastation but survival, and though these stories were told to me in confidence, I was encouraged by their bravery (that word again) to reach out to me. They seemed to break the unspoken code that some things are too terrible to discuss. They told me I could survive too. They gave me pieces of themselves through their stories, and made me feel less shame about what they assured me was an illness and not a flaw or sin. They prayed with me but they also told me to continue fighting with therapy and medication. The strength and acceptance those women showed me far outweighed the shame from my professor. These women refused to be defined by their illnesses, and I began to see myself as one of many in a long line of survivors.

Though I began to accept my illness, and learned to like things about myself, I'm not sure that I truly loved myself. I still tried to judge my own worth based on success in friendships and romance. I don't think I believed I was lovable. I was superficially smart and funny but terribly insecure about my own worth. I still allowed my depression to tell me that, despite the diagnosis, I wasn't just ill; I was innately flawed.

By 2005 I was outwardly very confident. I was at the start of realizing my dreams of studying to becoming a professor. It was a wonderful year; I met and fell in love with my husband at that time. I was with old and new friends, learning, and teaching, but I was still cutting. That's the main way I know I didn't truly love myself; I was still addicted to and relying on self-harm to vent my self-loathing.

Even though I stopped cutting in about 2006 with the help of my husband, I think it wasn't until 2012 that I finally committed to loving myself. During a very difficult period of my fifth depressive episode, I was at my parents' house having dinner with my family when my then-four-year-old niece prayed over our dinner, "Dear God, thank you for loving us even when we do bad things." I don't know why but that simple prayer was like a knife to my heart. I practically ran from the table in order to hide my tears. Was this small child right? Could God possibly love me despite my brokenness, despite the pain I caused to those around me? I still felt totally unlovable; I couldn't understand why my family loved me or treated me well. I felt like rabid Old Yeller—someone ought to take me to the shed and put me out of my misery. But maybe God was different. I had chosen to believe that He was omniscient, omnipresent, why not all-loving too?

My Bible memory is fuzzy from years of inactivity, but I remember that Jesus said the two greatest commandments are first to love God, and second to love your neighbor as yourself (Mark 12: 30-31). I could find reason to love God and others, but I couldn't love myself because of the destruction I seemed to cause. The thing is though, it's a commandment from Jesus, which meant I had the option to obey or disobey. I couldn't believe that Jesus would command me to do something impossible. I realized for the first time that self-love is a choice rather than some innate quality. If I didn't at least try to love myself—really give myself the benefit of the doubt—I was misunderstanding one of the most basic tenets of the faith I had chosen.

Of course it wasn't instantaneous, of course I still experience self-loathing. My depression did not disappear once I chose to try to love myself, but my perspective changed. The more love and acceptance I showed myself, the easier it was to accept it from others, and the easier it became to give it to others. I began to love myself too much to feel shame about what I knew was an illness. I began talking more openly about myself, less afraid of rejection. I wanted to be like those women who told me their stories of survival. I began to see the value in the battles I had fought.

And now? As I begin to feel my depression creeping closer, I feel compelled to speak. I won't let depression take from me what I have worked so hard to accept—my own self-worth. Depression may take everything, but I will fight until my last breath to be the woman I am. My struggle is just living, being, surviving, and that is enough. And if I can save one person from any of the despair I have felt, I must do it. If I am valuable, then all of you who suffer alongside me are also valuable. I can't let you go without telling you that. It's not ego, it's love, and if you feel it for yourself I believe you won't be able to keep from sharing it.

First I chose to love myself, then I had to learn how, and practice, practice, practice. I'm practicing right now. Every blog post is an acknowledgement of my value. My depression tells me it's all meaningless—worthless—but I won't listen, and maybe that's the brave part. If so, then I am one among many, and what I want is for you to join our ranks.

Don't be ashamed of who you are; don't let depression or other people tell you what your story is. I beg you to try to love yourself even though depression makes it seem impossible. You deserve love, especially from yourself. You matter; your journey matters. Keep fighting and I'll keep writing. We'll be brave together.

16

Changing Vows

MARRIAGE IS TOUGH, AND DEPRESSION IS TOUGH, BUT DEPRESSION IN MARRIAGE IS ITS OWN UNIQUE CHALLENGE. My husband and I have been married for seven years and had our first date ten years ago this month. That time also includes three depressive episodes; I was recovering from an episode during our wedding and have had two more since we said our vows. We wrote our own wedding vows, and I reread them this week. They're kind of adorable. They definitely sound like two romantic idealists in their mid-20s. It's only been seven years, but we have really changed; our understanding of what it means to commit to share your life with another adult has developed dramatically. I think about couples like my grandparents who have been married for more than 60 years, and I am blown away at the amount of knowledge they have gained over decades of commitment.

My husband and I firmly believe that individuals are constantly changing, requiring constant maneuvering, accommodation, and renegotiation. So when I look at our vows, I think about how naive we were. We said some things that only seven years of marriage have changed. We promised things we simply cannot do, but though the details may have changed, our commitment to each other and our ever-evolving partnership has not wavered. In 2008 we could not fathom how my severe depression (or any number of other events) would affect our marriage and change our vows, but we didn't need to know that yet. We just needed to be ready to begin a life together.

As an example, I want to look at just one of my husband's vows to me—"to bear your burdens as my own"—and expand upon how our perspective has developed as we have changed.

At the time of our wedding, I was recovering from my third depressive episode. My lowest point in the episode had been roughly four months prior, but I was still struggling to regain my health. During the lowest point, my husband had been living in Florida studying for his PhD, so my mother had been my primary caretaker when I could not live alone. My husband had experienced my depression mostly through the phone and weekend visits. He moved into my apartment two months before our wedding to help me recover, but he experienced only a fraction of the depths of my depression. So vowing to carry my burdens as his own seemed not only romantic but also possible. Based on what bits of my depression he had seen, he felt that he was ready to help me when necessary. By 2012 I was more deeply depressed than I had been since before our wedding. We had been through an episode together in 2010, but it hadn't been too bad. I had to drop out of school, but I hadn't been suicidal. But my fifth episode beginning in 2012 was different. I waited too long to ask for help, and I tried to hide my illness from my husband because he was working so hard. By the time I could no longer hide it, I was deeply depressed and overburdened with suicidal ideation. I still kept my thoughts to myself but my emotional upset poured out. A distance grew between us—a chasm of misunderstanding. He couldn't bear my burden; he may never even come close to understanding what it feels like. I ended up reaching out to my parents for help and eventually moved to Texas for four months to recover.

What we learned during that episode and our eventual time apart was that it would never work if we relied on my husband's ability to grasp my struggle. He couldn't simply share my burden the way we share finances. However, as we've changed both naturally and purposefully due to time and experience, we've learned that what he can do is carry me while I bear my burden. It's just like Sam and Frodo at the entrance of Mount Doom: when Frodo is practically paralyzed by the burden of the ring, Sam exclaims, "I can't carry it for you, but I can carry you." My husband realized that to make up for his inability to help me with my internal struggle, he must externally provide me with extra time, resources, and flexibility. Some burdens that we should share, he carries alone in order to give me the strength to fight my depression. He doesn't bear my burden as his own;

he does his best to lighten the rest of my load so that I can continue to better bear my heaviest burden. He works hard to supplement our tight budget since I have proven healthier without the stress of a job outside of the home. He takes the lead on certain chores because they cause me anxiety. He does my other jobs when I can only work to stay afloat.

I certainly don't regret my 27-year-old husband vowing to bear my burdens as his own—it was a meaningful pledge at the time—but I love that my 35-year-old husband has been willing to adjust to our ever-evolving knowledge of how depression affects our relationship. We are all constantly changing, and depression can cause dramatic change. My husband and I try to stay flexible and go with the flow, but in a purposeful and goal-oriented way. We are committed to our marriage and my health, and we are committed to remaining open to change in each other and our relationship.

17
The Battle of Self-Harm

IN 2001, AFTER MY FIRST BREAKDOWN, I MOVED OUT OF MY COLLEGE DORM ROOM AND BACK INTO MY PARENTS' HOUSE TO RECOVER. I was a complete mess at the time—newly diagnosed but deeply depressed. I still felt suicidal and desperate for a release from my pain. I was itching for a quick fix rather than the long journey ahead of me. In the late 1990s I had randomly come across an episode of 90210 with a side-storyline about a character cutting herself. Not being a 90210 fan, I didn't watch much, but I was fascinated by the cutting. It seemed so strange and foreign to me, but I did not forget; I stored the images in my brain for some later date.

In 2001 I remembered that strange, distressed character cutting herself on TV. I was in a great deal of emotional pain, full of self-loathing. No one would give me the physical punishment I felt I deserved, so finally I figured I would do it myself. I used a razor in the shower and cut my forearms multiple times—not that deep, but deep enough to cause a bit of the physical pain I felt I deserved. It also felt liberating to see wounds on my body; I felt that finally I would look as damaged as I felt. But I planned to keep it a secret; I knew my family, who had just spent 48 hours in the hospital with me, would be furious. I knew it was a bad idea to everyone else, but I felt relief when I cut. I planned to keep cutting regularly because of how it made me feel.

Not long after I started though, I was discovered. My family was on their way to the country club after church for lunch one Sunday when my sister noticed just a bit of one cut on my arm temporarily revealed when I pushed up my sleeve a bit in the car. She looked at me but said nothing in front of my parents. When we got our table she asked me to come to the bathroom with her. It had a large dressing area as well as a bathroom, so we sat alone in the dressing room in front of the giant mirrors and bright lights. She demanded to see my arms. After my initial refusal, I pulled up my sleeves. I will never forget—she immediately turned away, nauseous. Her reaction wasn't a rejection of me but she was overwhelmed and physically sickened by what I had done to myself. We pulled ourselves together to return to our table with my parents, but she told me that I had to tell my parents what I was doing today or she would.

Once we returned home from lunch, my family sat in the living room and I told them. They cried, my mother openly told me she had no idea what to do. She didn't know whether she was qualified to help me through this. She didn't know whether I could be helped at home or whether I needed inpatient therapy. I was afraid to spend time in a psychiatric hospital. I wanted to stay with my parents, but I did not want to give up cutting. I had only done it a few times over a couple of weeks, but I was hooked. It felt externally like I felt internally, it looked on the outside like I figured I looked on the inside—jagged, bleeding, wounded. But I didn't have much of a choice to continue unless I ran away from my family and the help they were providing me.

Quitting, even after such a short beginning, was difficult. I continually saw mental images of myself bleeding and I felt relief; then I felt compelled to follow through. My depression made me feel good about hurting myself; it seemed like a good thing. I would cut secretly whenever I got the chance. My parents stopped leaving me alone because I would cut if I got the chance. It got so bad that I had to share a bed with my mother (booting out my dad) so that I would not cut at night while they were asleep. They would check my arms and legs before bed to see how many cuts there were, then recount the next day to make sure there weren't more. They begged me to stop and made me tell my psychiatrist. My psychiatrist was not shocked; she had seen much worse cutting in her career. She told me the issue wasn't really the wounds but the desire and the addiction. The superficial wounds would easily heal with minor cleaning and bandaging; the problem was mental. My depression was still in control, and though I refused the desires to kill myself, I was giving in to the substitute desires to self-harm as a stopgap until my depression could lead me back to suicide.

It was difficult to stop; I craved to see my own blood; I wanted to scream my pain to everyone but I didn't know how. I felt like a visible wound was the most forthright way to communicate my distress. I stopped covering up my cuts for a time, which was embarrassing. The message I thought I was sending was met with confusion and repulsion. So I began doing a better job of hiding my cutting—using my thighs rather than my arms. I learned to control my cutting impulses until my parents began to ease up on me. When I regained my privacy, I began cutting again. One day about a year after I began, I had a panic attack at my job. I left work, drove to the drugstore, bought razors, and sat in my car sobbing and cutting. Two men jogging saw me and came to see whether I was alright. Terribly embarrassed, I made an excuse and drove away. I could see how crazy I was, but I didn't want to really quit cutting. Self-harm was like the ace up my sleeve. I could always fall back on it, but I also realized that I must keep it more secret than ever. I could not lose control and cut in public; I would be forced to stop if anyone found out. I cut off and on for the next few years, always keeping it in check so that no one would know. I only did it when I was in crisis to punish myself for my failings and receive relief from the invisibility of my pain.

It wasn't until 2006 that I finally gave it up. It was just a few months after meeting my husband, and I could not hide it from him. He saw when I would cut, and he would not tolerate it. He didn't threaten to leave me, but he refused to help me keep it a secret. For the first time, I decided to actually try to quit. I was recently heartbroken, newly in love, and happier than I had been in a while. I had refused to quit cutting with my previous boyfriend, and my depression contributed to our breakup. I didn't want depression to control my relationships the way it controlled the rest of my life. So I began telling my husband when I would feel the urge to cut rather than silently suffering through the temptation and eventually giving in. He would help distract me until the urge passed. Despite my doubts, the urge would pass. And the more times I resisted, the less the urge would come. I slipped up a few times early on, but my husband was gentle with me and encouraged me to just keep fighting.

At this point, I can't clearly remember the last time I cut, but I do remember the last time I wanted to. It was last week. I was driving down my street coming home from dropping my daughter off at school. I was feeling depressed and generally anxious, and the thought came to me loudly. And I just tossed it aside. I responded that I didn't do that any more, and it was gone. After that brief mental exchange I felt afraid but strong. I am still afraid of my depression and how deeply it has its claws in my brain, but I am proud of my ability of stand up to my depression and win even a momentary battle. A few years ago, an urge to cut could follow me around for days, but now it's easier to deal with. The temptation is still there, but I have a lot of experience saying no.

Self-harm is a dangerous business. Besides the harm you can potentially do to your body, you are feeding and nurturing your illness when you self-harm, and the less you feed it, the weaker it will become. Stopping self-harm will not cure your illness, but it will affect your ability to fight your illness. You may rationalize your self-harm, you may deeply believe you deserve it, or you may believe that it is the only way you can find relief from your pain. But there is more to this life than pain. You deserve healing rather than more hurt. Part of loving yourself is loving your body and treating it with gentleness. You are suffering enough; just because your illness is invisible to others does not mean it is any less real. Your value as a unique individual extends from your soul to your physical body. I beg that you treat both your body and brain with the love you deserve.

My story is just one of many recovering cutters. I've met others; you too can quit. Self-harm is a weapon that belongs to your mental illness, but you can disable that weapon by not giving in. I strongly suggest you find one or more true friends to help you quit. Tell them your problem and ask whether they will help keep you accountable. Tell your physician and counselor. Don't keep it a secret no matter how taboo. You deserve better.

Although I have not cut for years, I do have scars, mostly on my forearms. They are faded now, but I can still see them. They remind me of sitting in the bathroom of my parents' house, crying and cutting, hopeless. They remind me of the depths to which my depression takes me. I remember a woman approaching me at a restaurant and asking what had happened to me. I remember those two frightened men who found me in the parking lot. But every year the scars get fainter and the fight gets easier. I haven't been able to escape my depression, but I'm winning the battle against cutting. And in this war, every battle counts.

18
Saying Good-bye, Part 1

As I begin to feel better, I am finding myself rediscovering the positivity that seemed lost to me a couple of weeks ago. The best thing about this optimism is that it motivates me to work on my mental health. I am energized and able to look at myself with clearer vision. My counseling appointment last week benefitted from that energy and motivation. I was better able to listen and focus on what my counselor said to me. I have been able to let the appointment sink in. As a result, I have come to a conclusion. It is time for me to say good-bye to two specific thought patterns. By say good-bye, I mean that I must commit to never again, under my own strength, indulge them in any form. I made a similar break with cutting in 2006, but it is time again to seriously cut some things out of my life—specifically, monetary self-worth and suicidal ideation.

In 2012 I became obsessed with my value in terms of dollar amount. I began calculating the amount of food I ate and energy I used. I weighed my consumption against things like cost of childcare if I was no longer around to care for my daughter. I knew those dollar amounts didn't truly represent my value, but when faced with poverty and depression those dollars seemed so significant. Priceless qualities and contributions rang in at zero. I resumed calculating my worth a few weeks ago. The obsessive thinking about value in 2012 created well-traveled neural pathways in my brain that my depression willingly traveled again when I was not medicated. I now know that this is a tool that my depression will use against me if I let it, and I need to make a commitment to never calculate my worth in terms of money again. Any time I feel the urge, I must resist pulling out paper, pen, and calculator. I must resist the urge to budget or search for the cost of childcare. These things are not terribly difficult to commit to because they involve direct actions. If the thoughts come up, I just resist the desire by refusing to literally do the math. Like with cutting, the first step to stopping the desire is to refuse to do the action. Then the desire slowly loses control.

Saying good-bye to suicidal ideation is going to be far, far more difficult. I have been toying with it for at least 15 years. When I feel at my worst, it comforts me to know that there is at least one thing I can do to stop my pain. It seems a gift I can give my loved ones when I can give nothing else. It may seem incredibly strange, but part of me doesn't want to say good-bye. It's my last resort, and what do I have left if survival doesn't work? Part of me derives so much (false) peace from the resolve that my death will one day come at my own hand. I fear dying on any other terms. I use suicidal ideation as a way to avoid thinking about the fragility of all human life. It is deeply ingrained in my psyche. Saying good-bye means refocusing myself completely. As I write this I feel the weight of it. It is part of me, and I have to cut it off. If I choose to try to believe that I can one day be free of this burden, I must let go of this vague plan that relies on my continued illness. This good-bye must be significant—ceremonial even. I have to make a significant impression on myself in order to truly remember the moment of my commitment. I haven't decided how or when to do this, but I know it needs to happen.

19

Saying Good-bye, Part 2

IT'S A NEW YEAR, AND THIS TIME AROUND, I SORT OF FEEL NEW TOO. Early in December I did have a special date night with my husband to celebrate my commitment to reject suicidal thinking. We went out for a nice dinner, had champagne by the fire, and I wrote down some of my most prevalent suicidal thoughts and burned them. But I didn't feel happy about it; it wasn't even bittersweet. I felt a mixture of sadness, bitterness, and resignation. It was not what I was expecting. I hoped I would feel liberated, overjoyed, and strong. It was weird, but I made my commitment nonetheless. I have had very few suicidal thoughts since beginning my medication, but each time, since the beginning of December, I have pushed it aside and forcibly thought of something else. But I still haven't felt victorious.

I've been contemplating my feelings concerning my commitment, and I think I'm kind of grieving. I've cut off something I've held close for my entire adult life. For many years I held it so close that it was my biggest secret. Even as I began to talk openly about my past or present suicidal thoughts, I kept close my future plans to give in. And now I've let it go. I don't know whether it feels like amputating part of myself or murdering part of myself, but it feels violent. I've turned my back on a dear friend. Forever.

So what have I learned? This won't be easy. Every time I say no, I grieve the loss of my Virginia Woolf moment—the moment I save my loved ones from myself. But—and this is really important—that moment fully depends upon my resignation to my continued illness. I must believe that I will be suicidally ill again to believe that I will die by my own hand. And my real decision is not that I will not commit suicide, but that God will deliver me from this illness. That with medication, therapy, and hard work, I may be able to escape the ugly cycle of depressive episodes that has plagued me since 2000.

Because suicidal thinking has become habitual for me due to years of practice, I have decided to focus on being more intentional in my life. Every time a suicidal thought comes to me, I am intentional about pushing it away. I am also intentionally choosing to have faith in God's healing to provide me with hope, and I want to take that intentionality into other areas of my life. It's strange, but my commitment to saying good-bye to my suicidal plans despite my bitterness led me to this focus on intentionality. I chose positive action over negative feeling, which to me is a great success. If it had been easy or pleasurable to deny that part of myself, it wouldn't have made as much of an impact.

But I won't soon forget sitting beside my fireplace with a piece of paper. Written on the paper was my plan to kill myself in the distant future—my complete resignation to my illness. I reluctantly threw it in the fire as tears began to roll down my face. As I watched it burn my heart was aching. And then it was gone. But I'm still here and I'm still standing. God is good, I am so blessed, and for the first time in a while I feel real hope for the future.

20

How to Build a Life around Depression

TIME AND TIME AGAIN, DEPRESSION HAS CLOSED A DOOR FOR ME—GROWN UP AS AN UGLY BRUSH BLOCKING A PATH. First it took my college experience; fortunately, I was able to finish the second time around. Second, it took from me my ability to enjoy living alone. Next it took my career plans, and finally my original family plans. It has taken away my ability to handle high-stress situations and my ability to enjoy my daily blessings. At times it takes everything and I am left a struggling mess, but I continue to hang on. Why? Because sometimes I can see light. Sometimes I can see hope. I have been helped before, and I believe I can be helped again.

If you are going through your first episode, I beg you to rely on the success stories of others as evidence that not only are you not alone, but also that there is hope for you too. If you know what you are struggling with you have already won a battle in this war. If you think you might be depressed but aren't sure, I suggest you prioritize figuring that out. Read quality information on the Internet (I suggest the Mayo Clinic website), or better yet, make an appointment with your doctor. More than likely, you will be given a short written test with multiple-choice answers. Your score will be the first step in your doctor determining whether you are mildly or severely depressed. Then you can form a plan with your doctor.
If your doctor will not take your concerns of depression seriously, do not give up! Find a physician, counselor, or nurse practitioner—there are so many—who will listen to your concerns and help you formulate a plan for treatment.

If you have already been diagnosed or this is a subsequent episode for you, do not be discouraged—there is always hope of recovery. Statistically, my chances of complete recovery are slim, but I have now been mostly well since 2013 even though I had been through five episodes in the 13 years prior. Roughly three years of health. Five years ago that seemed impossible to me. I had tried so many things, but I continued to struggle. To be honest, I still struggle almost every day with my mental health, but I have routines, practices, and skills in place to keep me healthy.

So how have I built a life despite all that my depression

has taken from me? I have persevered, readjusted my goals and dreams, and prioritized myself.

Persevering

Facing any chronic illness takes perseverance because it is a continuous war of endurance against your ill body. Just like my daughter with Type 1 diabetes must persevere through all of her finger pokes, shots, blood draws, and other procedures, I must persevere through my mental crises by facing my need for medication and skills practice and acting on that need. With the help of your counselor, physician, or medical team, find—through trial and error—the right recipe of ingredients to balance your mental health. For me, this recipe involves daily medication, regular meditation, counseling, semiannual visits to a psychiatric specialist, lots of downtime and rest, intentional social engagement, and constant practice of behavioral skills I've learned through cognitive and dialectical behavioral training. The key to perseverance though, in my mind, is to live in the present with the knowledge that the present is temporary. By living in the present moment you can better practice mindfulness, which will do wonders for your mental health once you gain some mastery of it. You can appreciate the world around you, you can center yourself by focusing on your breathing, you can see what is literally in front of you. All of these effects of trying to mindfully live in the present can distract you from the tunnel thinking of depression, which lies to you about your current situation. If you are truly in a desperate place where the present doesn't give you any peace, remember that the present is always and only temporary. Things will change because that is the way life works. They may not change dramatically without action, but you may find opportunity and energy for action tomorrow. All you have to do is persevere through the present, knowing that it is temporary. As always, if you need help now, if you are in a desperate situation, please contact a medical provider, friend, family member, or the suicide prevention hotline. That is the action you can take in the present.

Readjusting Goals and Dreams

Does that sound awful? Shouldn't you pursue your dreams no matter the cost with a single-minded focus? I don't know, really, but I have chosen to readjust my goals and dreams rather than just mourn the loss of them or struggle with the near impossibility of them. I think a lot of happy adults have done this in life. It's one thing to just give up your dreams, but it is another to recognize that you change, life happens, and it is okay to change your goals as a result. As a teenager I wanted to be the mom of a big family. In college and grad school I decided to amend that dream by taking out a couple of kids and adding in a career as a college English professor. Once I was out of school and actually an adult, all of that seemed out of my reach. I had been through four depressive episodes. I had successfully gotten married and had an unplanned but graciously welcomed child, but I lived in an apartment and my husband was working himself to the bone trying to make enough money to pay our bills and work on his dissertation. Things seemed bleak for me. But things haven't been terrible since. As a teenager I wanted to be a stay-at-home mom; I am. As a college student I wanted to really spread my wings; moving from the South to the Pacific Northwest has been quite a geographical move. I wanted a family; I am in a fantastic partnership and have a truly unique child. I have two cats, one dog (soon to be two!), and a great rental house, and my husband is teaching composition and literature at a great university. I see myself as the queen of my empire. This little house on this little lot is full of love, laughter, and warmth, and I am queen of it! Sometimes I mourn what I've lost—specifically more children and a career—but usually I try to bask in what I've gained. My current dream is to continue to develop in this role and continue to be brave enough to take advantage of new opportunities. My goal is to make this home a happy place for my family. Though I stink at housework, I am great at spending quality time together. My goal is to keep us together, and I am succeeding. It isn't as awful as it sounds to readjust your focus. Anyway, the present holds so many surprises; to feel that you are doing your present role well and with purpose is fulfilling, and to be available to new opportunity gives you the chance to expand your present goals to incorporate the future.

Prioritizing Yourself

There is an important difference between prioritizing yourself and focusing on yourself. Depression makes you focus on your own problems and your inabilities. You see your flaws and your issues so clearly, but everything else is a blur. Sometimes you prioritize yourself by doing what is best for yourself, and often that means focusing on something besides what your depression wants you to focus on. You may feel that your thoughts are chaotic, but depressive thinking always takes you to the same destination—self-loathing. Take yourself out of this one-track thinking by prioritizing your health. Use mindfulness, meditation, journaling, distraction, or exercise to refocus yourself on something that is actually good for you.

Prioritizing yourself also means setting aside time specifically to work on your mental health. Not only does this include making time to take medication on a daily basis, but it also includes practicing skills, nutrition, exercise, rest, and sleep. It may include counseling, spirituality, intentional social time, immersion therapy, and many other things. A healthy day for me would include getting up at a the same time every day, going outside to be in (hopefully) sunlight, spending some time alone in the morning. Then I would get to my work for the day, including housework, homeschool work, writing, errands, appointments, and eating meals at the same time each day. In the late afternoon, I often take time for myself again or catch up on housework. Then after dinner I either spend time with my family or have date night with my husband. I attempt to do something social at least twice a week. I try to go to bed at the same time each day. Having a routine in place and doing things at roughly the same times each day will help regulate your body. I allow for plenty of flexibility in my schedule because I may wake up one morning unable to really do what needs to be done. I may not want to eat or work, so I will allow myself days to rest more because I would rather not lose control by pushing myself too hard. My routine involves lots of planning and scheduling with lots of flexibility. You may find that you need less planning or less flexibility. Your mix of work and rest will more than likely be different from mine, but it is important to find out the right mix for you and really try to prioritize maintaining that mix.

For most people, building a life is hard work. It takes

effort, flexibility, and focus. I have built a life around depression because I refused to let depression take my one life from me. I have continued to try, to readjust, to focus on my values and principles. I have learned to be myself, love myself, and care for myself. But it has taken a long time, and I am not complete, nor do I ever expect to be. Building a life is a process that continues as long as you live. Take it one day at a time, never underestimate the power of positivity, and reach out for help when you need it. You are valuable, and you deserve a wonderful life.

EPILOGUE
Who I Am

WHEN MY STRUGGLES WITH DEPRESSION BEGAN IN THE LATE 1990S, I BECAME INCREASINGLY UNSURE OF WHO I WAS. I could describe myself in relation to people, places, or activities, but I did not understand who I was apart from everything surrounding me. I felt like I was living a lie, that everything I said and did was programmed into me by everything I had learned at home, church, and school. For most of my life, adhering to the ideologies that had been presented to me as "right" was enough. But by my late teen years, I began to feel empty. I could repeat all the "right" answers, but I had no idea what it meant to actually believe in something. As a child, my world had seemed so small and safe. As I got older, the world got bigger, and I knew less and less. Everyone had seemed the same and now there were vast differences. People had different passions, ideas, values, and I only had a small portion of information. I felt afraid of the world and my place in it. I began to loathe what I saw as my inability to fit in. I didn't want the life I thought I had been raised to live. I wanted to learn more. Try new things. I wanted choices. I believed that if I did not know who I was with the knowledge I had on hand that I had better get more knowledge.

Unfortunately I was also desperately depressed by the time I had really begun to process these feelings. I felt out of place, and worse, that there was no place for me. I had to either be exactly the person my friends, family, teachers, and mentors wanted me to be *or* I had to die. I so hated being stuck in that situation that I chose to die. I refused to be someone I was not, and I refused to be stopped on my journey to self-discovery. But my depression made me believe that the only way I could fully escape was through death. Little did I know that my family and real friends only wanted me to be happy. They were willing to lose the pieces of myself that I no longer wanted because they loved me unconditionally. As a 19-year-old though, I saw no way out.

I have mentioned before that I credit my parents with saving my life in more ways than one. They literally saved my life the day I tried to kill myself; they saved my life by moving me in with them and caring for me when I was unable to care for myself; and they saved my life by finding me good, expert help. It is through counseling that I have really learned how to discover myself. It has given me the opportunity to work through my thoughts and feelings. Process my emotional reactions and thought patterns. I began to know myself by understanding how I worked. I learned about how depression worked, and I learned about what interested me. I tried new things, I read new books, I made new friends, I traveled to new places, I pushed myself to do things that I wanted to do even if I didn't receive resounding approval, and more importantly, I learned that I didn't need others' approval. As long as my health remained in check, I could live a life that made me happy. I stopped going to church, I started wearing really dark eye makeup, I started smoking, but I also started painting, I got a job, I traveled overseas by myself. I made some mistakes, but I learned quite a lot about the world and myself. I credit my parents with letting me do these things in search of myself. It must have been difficult to watch their mentally ill daughter try to find her way, but they were committed to my happiness and health.

This process of knowing myself has continued since I began my journey 15 years ago. I have actively sought to discover what I like, how I react, and what I need. I live without much anger or guilt. I continue to work on my fears. I make decisions for my life with confidence because I know that I am the most qualified person to make those decisions—and as a chronic depressive, that is not a small accomplishment.

From 2001–2008, I made great strides in my goal to know and understand myself. During that time I had earned my bachelor's degree and was working on my master's degree. I had been able to travel and study while making friends, although I had suffered with my depression off an on. I felt that I finally understood Laura Grace Dykes—the unique being known by that name. So when I got married in 2008, I was quite resistant to changing my name. Yes, I am a feminist, and I feel that women should do whatever they want with their names, but my desire to keep my name was less political. I had worked hard over the past few years to understand Laura Grace Dykes, and now that I knew her, I didn't want her to change. It is silly, I know, because it is just a name, but I felt like changing my name wouldn't give my hard work the acknowledgment it deserved. And eight years later I am still very pleased with my decision. I still feel that my name is the best label for me, and if I changed it I wouldn't love it quite as much because I wouldn't remember all the work and struggle behind owning it.

I really believe that change is inevitable, but I also believe that a person can know herself even as she changes. It's about riding the waves of change with centered confidence rather than standing still. I never thought that I would end up living and loving the Pacific Northwest. I am a Southern girl born and bred, but I am so happy up here in the Evergreen State. I love the mountains, the water, the trees, the people. I love being so close to Seattle that I can go whenever I want. These are things I never could have predicted for myself. I am the parent of an only child. Growing up, I prejudicially thought that all children should have siblings. Now I better understand other single-child families, and I am happy that I knew myself enough to know that I could not risk having another baby due to the hormonal changes, risk of postpartum depression, added stress, lack of rest, etc. I am trying to stay healthy, and I know that I am happy and fulfilled with the family I have built, and that they need me to stay as healthy as possible. It hasn't been easy to commit to the decision to not have more children, but when I feel sad about it, I remember who I am now, what I have, and why I have made the decisions I have made, and I always leave the moment feeling that I have made the right decision for me. I must acknowledge that I am a strong-enough woman to know what is best for my life and follow through on my self-knowledge rather than only listening to outside opinions.

I don't really know whether identity is centered just in the brain, or whether it is partially in the soul, and I'm not sure whether intuition is real or whether the Holy Spirit guides us through our decisions, but I do believe that it is possible to know yourself in this moment even if you are a different person the next. Taking time for self-discovery, following my passions while prioritizing my health, and being confident while facing inevitable change have all helped me build a strong identity, a strong sense of self. I like who I am. I like my quirks, my oddities, my strength, my talents. I like how I look, where I live, who I spend my time with, and how I act. I'm not at all perfect, and I am grateful that I have the opportunity to learn from my mistakes. As always, I am greatly indebted to family, friends, counselors, and psychiatrists who have helped me get to this point over the past 15 years. And I am still—daily—learning new things about myself with the help of my husband, daughter, friends, and counselor. It is never ending, and that excites me. I love who I am, and I hope that that love just continues to grow. I want to be stronger, braver, more loving, more intentional. I want to face change with strength and grace. I want to continue to discover myself as I inevitably change with time and circumstance.

Finally, I hope that you have noticed that I have not allowed my identity to be found in my depression. I acknowledge (gratefully, actually) its major impact on who I have become—it has given me strength and compassion—but I refuse to be defined by my horrible illness. I am a result of my circumstances, but I have a choice in who I choose to be and how I choose to view myself. Depression will always be part of me, but I refuse to let it consume me or my identity when I have the power to push it away. When I can't see beyond the depression, I remember—always remember—that the pain is temporary. Tomorrow is another day with new chances for help or change. You are valuable, you are unique, you are irreplaceable. You deserve love from others, but most importantly, you deserve love from yourself. I encourage you to get to know yourself and gently love who you are right now. Prioritize your health and happiness, and enjoy the journey.

Made in the USA
Middletown, DE
27 September 2017